W9-CEJ-951

God's Answers to Your Questions

A Quick Reference to Bible Topics

Abridged from
Bible Readings for the Home

REVIEW AND HERALD® PUBLISHING ASSOCIATION
HAGERSTOWN, MD 21740

Third edition
Copyright © CMCMXIV, MCMXXXV, MCMXLII, MCMCLIX, MCMLVII, MCMLXII
and MCMLXXXIX by
Review and Herald® Publishing Association
International copyright secured

This book was
Edited by Tim Crosby
Designed by Bill Kirstein
HHES cover art by John Robinette
FHES cover design by Reger Smith, Jr.
Typeset: 9.5/10 Times

PRINTED IN U.S.A.

FHES ISBN 0-8280-1440-X

05   15

CONTENTS

Good News About
THE FUTURE

THE KING'S DREAM

What statement did Nebuchadnezzar, king of Babylon, make to his wise men whom he had assembled?

"And the king said unto them, *I have dreamed a dream, and my spirit was troubled to know the dream."* Daniel 2:3.

After being threatened with death if they did not make known the dream and the interpretation, what did the wise men say to the king?

"The Chaldeans answered before the king, and said, *There is not a man upon the earth that can shew the king's matter:* therefore there is no king, lord, nor ruler, that asked such things at any magician, or astrologer, or Chaldean. And it is a rare thing that the king requireth, and *there is none other that can shew it before the king, except the gods, whose dwelling is not with flesh."* Verses 10, 11.

After the wise men had thus confessed their inability to do what the king required, who offered to interpret the dream?

"Then *Daniel* went in, and desired of the king that he would give him time, and that he would shew the king the interpretation." Verse 16.

After Daniel and his fellows had sought God earnestly, how were the dream and its interpretation revealed to Daniel?

"Then was the secret revealed unto Daniel *in a night vision.* Then Daniel blessed the God of heaven." Verse 19.

When brought before the king, what did Daniel say?

"Daniel answered in the presence of the king, and said, The secret which the king hath demanded cannot the wise men, the astrologers, the magicians, the soothsayers, shew unto the king; but *there is a God in heaven that revealeth secrets,* and maketh known to the king Nebuchadnezzar what shall be in the latter days. Thy dream, and the visions of thy head upon thy bed, are these." Verses 27, 28.

THE GREAT IMAGE

What did Daniel say the king had seen in his dream?

"Thy dream, and the visions of thy head upon thy bed, are these; . . . Thou, O king, sawest, and behold *a great image.* This great image, whose brightness was excellent, stood before thee; and the form thereof was terrible." Verses 28-31.

Of what were the different parts of the image composed?

"This image's head was of fine *gold,* his breast and his arms of *silver,* his belly and his thighs of *brass,* his legs of *iron,* his feet *part of iron and part of clay."* Verses 32, 33.

By what means was the image broken to pieces?

"Thou sawest till that *a stone* was cut out without hands, which smote the image upon his feet that were of iron and clay, and brake them to pieces." Verse 34.

What became of the various parts of the image?

"Then was the iron, the clay, the brass, the silver, and the gold, broken to pieces together, and *became like the chaff of the summer threshingfloors; and the wind carried them away,* that no place was found for them: and the stone that smote the image became a great mountain, and filled the whole earth." Verse 35.

DANIEL AND THE INTERPRETATION

With what words did Daniel begin the interpretation of the dream?

"Thou, O king, art a king of kings: for the God of heaven hath given thee a kingdom, power, and strength, and glory. And wheresoever the children of men dwell, the beasts of the field and the fowls of the heaven hath he given into thine hand, and hath made thee ruler over them all. *Thou art this head of gold."* Verses 37, 38.

NOTE—The character of the Neo-Babylonian Empire is fittingly indicated by the nature of the material composing that portion of the image by which it was symbolized—the head of gold. It was "the golden kingdom of a golden age." The metropolis, Babylon, as enlarged and beautified during the reign of Nebuchadnezzar, reached a height of unrivaled magnificence. The ancient writers, like Herodotus, are found by archaeologists to be generally accurate, except for a tendency to exaggerate as to size in their enthusiastic descriptions of the great city with its massive fortifications, its lavishly ornamented temples and palaces, its lofty temple-tower, and its "hanging gardens" rising terrace upon terrace, which came to be known among the Greeks as one of the seven wonders of the ancient world.

What was to be the nature of the next kingdom after Babylon?

"After thee shall arise another kingdom *inferior to thee.*" Verse 39, first part.

Who was the last Babylonian king?

"In that night was *Belshazzar* the king of the Chaldeans slain. And Darius the Median took the kingdom, being about threescore and two years old." Daniel 5:30, 31. (See also verses 1, 2.)

To whom was Belshazzar's kingdom given?

"Thy kingdom is divided, and given to *the Medes and Persians.*" Verse 28.

By what is this kingdom of the Medes and Persians, generally known as the Persian Empire, represented in the great image?

The breast and arms of *silver.* (Daniel 2:32.)

By what is the Greek, or Macedonian, Empire, which succeeded the kingdom of the Medes and Persians, represented in the image?

"His belly and his thighs of *brass.*" Verse 32. "And another *third kingdom of brass,* which shall bear rule over all the earth." Verse 39.

NOTE—That the empire which replaced the Persian was the Greek is clearly stated in Daniel 8:5-8, 20, 21.

What is said of the fourth kingdom?

"And the fourth kingdom *shall be strong as iron:* forasmuch as iron breaketh in pieces and subdueth all things: and as iron that breaketh all these, *shall it break in pieces and bruise.*" Daniel 2:40.

What scripture shows that the Roman emperors ruled the world?

"And it came to pass in those days, that *there went out a decree from Caesar Augustus, that all the world should be taxed.*" Luke 2:1.

NOTE—Describing the Roman conquests, Gibbon uses the very imagery employed in the vision of Daniel 2. He says: "The arms of the republic, sometimes vanquished in battle, always victorious in war, advanced with rapid steps to the Euphrates, the Danube, the Rhine, and the ocean; and the images of gold or silver, or brass, that might serve to represent the nations and their kings, were successively broken by the iron monarchy of Rome."—*The History of the Decline and Fall of the Roman Empire,* chap. 38, par. 1, under "General Observations," at the close of the chapter.

MAN'S FAILURE TO UNITE NATIONS

What was indicated by the mixture of clay and iron in the feet and toes of the image?

"And whereas thou sawest the feet and toes, part of potters' clay, and part of iron, *the kingdom shall be divided.*" Daniel 2:41.

NOTE—The barbarian tribes that overran the Roman Empire formed the kingdoms which developed into the nations of modern Europe.

Were any efforts to be made to reunite the divided empire of Rome?

"And whereas thou sawest iron mixed with miry clay, *they shall mingle themselves with the seed of men:* but they shall not cleave one to another, even as iron is not mixed with clay." Verse 43.

NOTE—Charlemagne, Charles V, Louis XIV, Napoleon, Kaiser Wilhelm, and Hitler all tried to reunite the broken fragments of the Roman Empire and failed. By marriage and intermarriage of royalty ties have been formed with a view to strengthening and cementing together the shattered kingdom, but none have succeeded. The element of disunion remains. Many political revolutions and territorial changes have occurred in Europe since the end of the Western Roman Empire in A.D. 476; but its divided state still remains.

What is to take place in the days of these kingdoms?

"And in the days of these kings shall *the God of heaven set up a kingdom, which shall never be destroyed: . . . but it shall break in pieces and consume all these kingdoms, and it shall stand for ever.*" Verse 44.

NOTE—This verse foretells the establishment of another universal kingdom, the kingdom of God. This kingdom is to overthrow and supplant all existing earthly kingdoms, and is to stand forever. The time for the setting up of this kingdom was to be "in the days of these kings." This cannot refer to the four preceding empires, or kingdoms, for they were not contemporaneous, but successive; neither can it refer to an establishment of the kingdom at Christ's first advent, for the ten kingdoms which arose out of the ruins of the Roman Empire were not yet in existence. This final kingdom, then, is yet future.

In what announcement in the New Testament is the establishment of the kingdom of God made known?

"And the seventh angel sounded; and there were great voices in heaven, saying, *The kingdoms of this world are become the kingdoms of our Lord, and of his Christ;* and he shall reign for ever and ever." Revelation 11:15.

King Nebuchadnezzar's Dream
Jim Padgett, Artist

Good News About
THE BIBLE

By what name are the sacred writings of the Bible commonly known?

"Jesus saith unto them, Did ye never read in *the scriptures,* The stone which the builders rejected, the same is become the head of the corner?" Matthew 21:42.

What other title is given this revelation of God to man?

"And he answered and said unto them, My mother and my brethren are these which hear *the word of God,* and do it." Luke 8:21.

NOTE—It is interesting to note that the word *Bible* does not occur in the Bible itself. It is derived from the Latin *biblia,* which came from the Greek *biblos,* meaning "book." The Greek word *biblos* in turn is derived from *byblos,* meaning "papyrus," the name of the material upon which ancient books were written. The Greeks called this writing material *byblos* because they obtained it from the Phoenician port of Byblos.

The Bible has 66 books and was written by 35 or 40 men over a period of some 1,500 years. The books are called the "Word of God," or the "Scriptures." *Scriptures* means "writings."

THE MANNER IN WHICH THE SCRIPTURES WERE GIVEN

How were the Scriptures given?

"All scripture is given *by inspiration of God."* 2 Timothy 3:16.

By whom were the men directed who thus spoke for God?

"For the prophecy came not in old time by the will of man: but holy men of God spake as they were moved *by the Holy Ghost."* 2 Peter 1:21.

What specific instance is mentioned by Peter?

"Men and brethren, this scripture must needs have been fulfilled, *which the Holy Ghost by the mouth of David spake before concerning Judas,* which was guide to them that took Jesus." Acts 1:16.

Who, therefore, did the speaking through these men?

"God, who at sundry times and in divers manners spake in time past unto the fathers by the prophets." Hebrews 1:1.

THE PURPOSE OF THE SCRIPTURES

For what purpose were the Scriptures written?

"For whatsoever things were written aforetime were written *for our learning,* that we through patience and comfort of the scriptures might have hope." Romans 15:4.

For what is all Scripture profitable?

"All scripture is given by inspiration of God, and is profitable *for doctrine, for reproof, for correction, for instruction in righteousness."* 2 Timothy 3:16.

What was God's design in thus giving the Scriptures?

"That the man of God may be *perfect, throughly furnished unto all good works."* Verse 17.

What does God design that His Word shall be to us in this world of darkness, sin, and death?

"Thy word is a *lamp* unto my feet, and a *light* unto my path." Psalm 119:105.

THE DIVISIONS OF THE SCRIPTURES

What three general divisions did Jesus refer to in the writings of the Old Testament?

"And he said unto them, These are the words which I spake unto you, while I was yet with you, that all things must be fulfilled, which were written in *the law of Moses,* and in *the prophets,* and in *the psalms,* concerning me." Luke 24:44.

NOTE—"The law of Moses" was a common Jewish term for the first five books of the Old Testament. In "the prophets" they included Isaiah, Jeremiah, Ezekiel, and the 12 Minor Prophets; also Joshua, Judges, 1 and 2 Samuel, and 1 and 2 Kings. "The psalms" included all the remaining books.

Upon what evidence did Jesus base His Messiahship?

"And beginning at *Moses* and all the *prophets,* he expounded unto them *in all the scriptures* the things concerning himself." Verse 27.

NOTE—Jesus referred particularly to the Old Testament prophecies as proof of His Messiahship. When Christ spoke of the Scriptures, He meant the Old Testament, for the New Testament had not yet been written.

THE CHARACTER OF GOD AND HIS WORD

What is God called in the Scriptures?

"He is the Rock, his work is perfect: for all his ways are judgment: *a God of truth* and without iniquity, just and right is he." Deuteronomy 32:4.

What, therefore, must be the character of His word?

"Sanctify them through thy truth: *thy word is truth.*" John 17:17.

To what extent has God magnified His word?

"Thou hast magnified thy word *above all thy name.*" Psalm 138:2.

NOTE—A man's name stands for his character. It is the same with God. When God places His word above His name, His character becomes the foundation of His word and the pledge that His word will be fulfilled. (Hebrews 6:13, 14.)

THE TESTIMONY OF JOB AND ISAIAH

What estimate did Job place upon the words of God?

"Neither have I gone back from the commandment of his lips; *I have esteemed the words of his mouth more than my necessary food.*" Job 23:12.

How firm was the faith of the great Isaiah in the word of God?

"The grass withereth, the flower fadeth: but *the word of our God shall stand for ever.*" Isaiah 40:8.

THE POWER OF GOD'S WORD IN NATURE

Through what agency did God create the heavens?

"By the word of the Lord were the heavens made; and all the host of them *by the breath of his mouth. . . .* For *he spake,* and it was done; *he commanded,* and it stood fast." Psalm 33:6-9.

By what does Christ uphold all things?

"Upholding all things *by the word of his power.*" Hebrews 1:3.

Of what are some willingly ignorant?

"For this they willingly are ignorant of, that *by the word of God the heavens were of old,* and the earth standing out of the water and in the water: *whereby the world that then was, being overflowed with water, perished.*" 2 Peter 3:5, 6.

By what are the present heavens and earth reserved for a similar fate?

"But the heavens and the earth, which are now, *by the same word* are kept in store, reserved unto fire against the day of judgment and perdition of ungodly men." Verse 7.

In what other scripture is it shown that creative power is exercised through the word of God?

"Let them praise the name of the Lord: *for he commanded, and they were created.*" Psalm 148:5.

POWER OF GOD'S WORD IN REDEMPTION

What change is wrought in one who is in Christ?

"Therefore if any man be in Christ, *he is a new creature* [literally, *"a new creation,"* RV, margin]: old things are passed away; behold, *all things are become new.*" 2 Corinthians 5:17.

In what other words is this experience described by Jesus?

"Jesus answered and said unto him, Verily, verily, I say unto thee, Except a man be *born again,* he cannot see the kingdom of God." John 3:3.

Through what agency is this new creation, or new birth, accomplished?

"Being born again, not of corruptible seed, but of incorruptible, *by the word of God,* which liveth *and abideth for ever.*" 1 Peter 1:23.

NATURAL AND SPIRITUAL LIGHT COMPARED

What is the first creative commandment recorded in the Bible? and what was the result of it?

"And God said, *Let there be light:* and *there was light.*" Genesis 1:3.

What connection is there between the creation of light in the beginning, and the light of the gospel?

"For God, who commanded the light to shine out of darkness, hath shined in our hearts, to give *the light of the knowledge of the glory of God in the face of Jesus Christ.*" 2 Corinthians 4:6.

AMAZING POWER OF THE WORD SPOKEN

Why were the people astonished at Christ's teaching?

"And they were astonished at his doctrine: *for his word was with power.*" Luke 4:32.

What testified to the power of the word of Christ?

"And they were all amazed, and spake among themselves, saying, What a word is this! for *with authority and power he commandeth the unclean spirits, and they come out.*" Verse 36.

How did God heal His people anciently?

"He sent his word, and healed them, and delivered them from their destructions." Psalm 107:20.

THE BIBLE

How did the centurion show his faith in Christ?

"The centurion answered and said, Lord, I am not worthy that thou shouldest come under my roof: but *speak the word only, and my servant shall be healed."* Matthew 8:8.

THE SEED OF GOD'S WORD WORKING IN US

What did Christ say is the seed of the kingdom of God?

"The seed is *the word of God."* Luke 8:11.

Where should the word of Christ dwell?

"Let the word of Christ *dwell in you* richly in *all wisdom."* Colossians 3:16.

What did Christ say of the unbelieving Jews respecting the word of God?

"Ye have not his word abiding in you: for whom he hath sent, him ye believe not." John 5:38.

How does the word of God work in the believer?

"For this cause also thank we God without ceasing, because, when ye received the word of God which ye heard of us, ye received it not as the word of men, but as it is in truth, the word of God, *which effectually worketh also in you that believe."* 1 Thessalonians 2:13.

HEART RESULTS OF GOD'S WORD

What nature is imparted through the promises of God?

"Whereby are given unto us exceeding great and precious promises: *that by these ye might be partakers of the divine nature,* having escaped the corruption that is in the world through lust." 2 Peter 1:4.

By what are believers made clean?

"Now ye are clean *through the word which I have spoken unto you."* John 15:3.

How does David say that a young man may cleanse his way?

"Wherewithal shall a young man cleanse his way? *by taking heed thereto according to thy word."* Psalm 119:9.

What power has the word when hidden in the heart?

"Thy word have I hid in mine heart, *that I might not sin against thee."* Psalm 119:11. (See also Psalm 17:4.)

GENERAL REFERENCES TO CHRIST

Of whom did Christ say the Scriptures testify?

"Search the scriptures; for in them ye think ye have eternal life: and *they are they which testify of me."* John 5:39.

NOTE—"Search the Old Testament Scriptures: for they are they that testify of Christ. To find Him in them is the true and legitimate end of their study. To be able to interpret them as He interpreted them is the best result of all Biblical learning."—DEAN ALFORD.

Of whom did Moses and the prophets write?

"Philip findeth Nathanael, and saith unto him, We have found him, of whom Moses in the law, and the prophets, did write, *Jesus of Nazareth,* the son of Joseph." John 1:45.

NOTE—In her translation of the Old Testament Scriptures, Helen Spurrell expressed the following wish for all who should read her translation: "May very many exclaim, as the translator has often done when studying numerous passages in the original, *I have found the Messiah!"*

From whose words did Christ say the disciples ought to have learned of His death and resurrection?

"O fools, and slow of heart to believe all that *the prophets* have spoken: ought not Christ to have suffered these things, and to enter into his glory?" Luke 24:25, 26.

How did Christ make it clear to them that the Scriptures testify of Him?

"And beginning at Moses and all the prophets, *he expounded unto them in all the scriptures the things concerning himself."* Verse 27.

CHRIST THE SEED

Where do we find the first promise of a Redeemer?

"And the Lord God said unto the serpent, . . . I will put enmity between thee and the woman, and between thy seed and *her seed;* it shall bruise thy head, and thou shalt bruise his heel." Genesis 3:14, 15.

In what words was this promise renewed to Abraham?

"In thy seed shall all the nations of the earth be blessed." Genesis 22:18. (See also Genesis 26:4; 28:14.)

To whom did this promised seed refer?

"Now to Abraham and his seed were the promises made. He saith not, And to seeds, as of many; but as of one, And to thy seed, *which is Christ."* Galatians 3:16.

THE ANGEL AND THE ROCK

Whom did God promise to send with Israel to guide them into the Promised Land?

"Behold, I send *an Angel* before thee, to keep thee

11

The Greatest Book in the World

Mitchell Heinze, Artist
© 1989 R&H

in the way, and to bring thee into the place which I have prepared." Exodus 23:20.

Who was the Rock that went with them?

"And did all drink the same spiritual drink: for they drank of that spiritual Rock that followed ["went with," margin] them: and *that Rock was Christ."* 1 Corinthians 10:4.

BIRTH, LIFE, SUFFERING, DEATH, RESURRECTION

Where was the Saviour to be born?

"But thou, *Bethlehem* Ephratah, though thou be little among the thousands of Judah, *yet out of thee shall he come forth* unto me that is to be ruler in Israel; whose goings forth have been from of old, from everlasting." Micah 5:2.

In what prophecy are Christ's life, suffering, and death touchingly foretold?

In the fifty-third chapter of Isaiah.

Where is the price of Christ's betrayal foretold?

"So they weighed for my price *thirty pieces of silver."* Zechariah 11:12. (See Matthew 26:15.)

Where in the Psalms are Christ's dying words recorded?

"My God, my God, why hast thou forsaken me?" Psalm 22:1. (See Matthew 27:46.) "Into thine hand I commit my spirit." Psalm 31:5. (See Luke 23:46.)

How is Christ's resurrection foretold in the Psalms?

"For *thou wilt not leave my soul in hell;* neither wilt thou suffer thine Holy One to see corruption." Psalm 16:10. (See Acts 2:25-31.)

CHRIST'S SECOND COMING AND KINGDOM

In what words does Daniel foretell Christ's receiving His kingdom?

"I saw in the night visions, and, behold, one like *the Son of man* came with the clouds of heaven, and came to the Ancient of days, and they brought him near before him. And *there was given him dominion, and glory, and a kingdom,* that all people, nations, and languages, should serve him: his dominion is an everlasting dominion, which shall not pass away, and his kingdom that which shall not be destroyed." Daniel 7:13, 14. (See also Luke 1:32, 33; 19:11, 12; Revelation 11:15.)

How is Christ's second coming described in the Psalms?

"Let the floods clap their hands: let the hills be joyful together before the Lord; *for he cometh to judge the earth:* with righteousness shall he judge the world, and the people with equity." Psalm 98:8, 9. *"Our God shall come, and shall not keep silence:* a fire shall devour before him, and it shall be very tempestuous round about him. He shall call to the heavens from above, and to the earth, that he may judge his people. Gather my saints together unto me; those that have made a covenant with me by sacrifice." Psalm 50:3-5.

Good News About
GOD

What two basic characteristics are part of God's nature?

"The Lord is *righteous* in all his ways, and *holy* in all his works." Psalm 145:17.

Does Christ possess these same attributes?

"By his knowledge shall *my righteous servant* [Christ] justify many." Isaiah 53:11. "Neither wilt thou suffer *thine Holy One* to see corruption." Acts 2:27.

In what language is the justice of God described?

"He is the Rock, his work is perfect: for *all his ways are judgment:* a God of truth and without iniquity, *just and right is he.*" Deuteronomy 32:4.

HIS STRENGTH, WISDOM, AND FAITHFULNESS

What is said of the strength and wisdom of God?

"Behold, God is *mighty,* and despiseth not any: he is *mighty in strength and wisdom.*" Job 36:5.

What treasures are hid in Christ?

"In whom are hid all the treasures of *wisdom* and *knowledge.*" Colossians 2:3.

What is said of God's faithfulness in keeping His promises?

"Know therefore that the Lord thy God, he is God, *the faithful God,* which keepeth covenant and mercy with them that love him and keep his commandments to a thousand generations." Deuteronomy 7:9.

THE LOVE AND COMPASSION OF GOD

In what one word is the character of God expressed?

"He that loveth not knoweth not God; for God is *love."* 1 John 4:8.

What is said of the tender compassion of God?

"But thou, O Lord, art a God *full of compassion,* and gracious, longsuffering, and plenteous in mercy and truth." Psalm 86:15.

HIS GRACIOUS IMPARTIALITY

In what words is His impartiality proclaimed?

"For the Lord your God is God of gods, and Lord of lords, a great God, a mighty, and a terrible, *which regardeth not persons,* nor taketh reward." Deuteronomy 10:17. "Then Peter opened his mouth, and said, Of a truth I perceive that *God is no respecter of persons:* but in every nation he that feareth him, and worketh righteousness, is accepted with him." Acts 10:34, 35.

To how many is the Lord good?

"The Lord is *good to all:* and his tender mercies are over all his works." Psalm 145:9.

Why did Christ tell us to love our enemies?

"But I say unto you, Love your enemies, bless them that curse you, do good to them that hate you, and pray for them which despitefully use you, and persecute you; *that ye may be the children of your Father which is in heaven: for he maketh his sun to rise on the evil and on the good, and sendeth rain on the just and on the unjust.*" Matthew 5:44, 45.

CHRIST'S CALL TO HIS PEOPLE

How perfect does Christ tell His followers to be?

"Be ye therefore perfect, *even as your Father which is in heaven is perfect.*" Verse 48.

What is God declared to be?

"God is *love."* 1 John 4:16.

How great is God's love for the world?

"For God so loved the world, that he gave his only begotten Son, that whosoever believeth in him should not perish, but have everlasting life." John 3:16.

In what act especially has God's love been manifested?

"In this was manifested the love of God toward us, because that *God sent his only begotten Son into the world, that we might live through him."* 1 John 4:9.

GOD'S DELIGHT

In what does God delight?

"Who is a God like unto thee, that pardoneth iniquity, and passeth by the transgression of the remnant of his heritage? he retaineth not his anger for ever, because *he delighteth in mercy."* Micah 7:18.

How are the mercies of Heaven continually manifested to the sons of men?

"It is of the Lord's mercies that we are not consumed, because his compassions fail not. *They are new every morning:* great is thy faithfulness." Lamentations 3:22, 23.

Upon how many does God bestow His blessings?

"He maketh his sun to rise on the evil and on the good, and sendeth rain on the just and on the unjust." Matthew 5:45.

In view of God's great love, what may we confidently expect?

"He that spared not his own Son, but delivered him up for us all, how shall he not with him also freely *give us all things?"* Romans 8:32.

FELLOWSHIP, SONSHIP, AND TRUST

What did Jesus say of the one who loves Him?

"He that loveth me shall be loved of my Father, and I will love him, and will manifest myself to him." John 14:21.

Into what relationship to God does His love bring us?

"Behold, what manner of love the Father hath bestowed upon us, that we should be called *the sons of God."* 1 John 3:1.

As sons of God, to what will we submit? How may we know that we are the sons of God?

"For *as many as are led by the Spirit of God,* they are the sons of God. . . . *The Spirit itself beareth witness with our spirit,* that we are the children of God." Romans 8:14-16.

How is the love of God supplied to the believer?

"And hope maketh not ashamed; because the love of God is shed abroad in our hearts *by the Holy Ghost* which is given unto us." Romans 5:5.

FELLOWSHIP OF BELIEVERS

In view of God's great love to us, what ought we to do?

"Beloved, if God so loved us, *we ought also to love one another."* 1 John 4:11.

With what measure of love should we serve others?

"Hereby perceive we the love of God, because he laid down his life for us: and *we ought to lay down our lives for the brethren."* 1 John 3:16.

What exhortation is based upon Christ's love for us?

"And *walk in love,* as Christ also hath loved us, and hath given himself for us an offering and a sacrifice to God for a sweetsmelling savour." Ephesians 5:2.

LOVE'S WISE WAY

Upon what ground does God's work for sinners rest?

"But God, who is rich in mercy, *for his great love wherewith he loved us,* even when we were dead in sins, hath quickened us together with Christ, (by grace ye are saved;) and hath raised *us up together, and made us sit together* in heavenly places in Christ Jesus." Ephesians 2:4-6. (See Titus 3:5, 6.)

In what other way is God's love sometimes shown?

"For whom the Lord loveth he *chasteneth,* and *scourgeth* every son whom he receiveth." Hebrews 12:6.

LOVE EVERLASTING

How enduring is God's love for us?

"The Lord hath appeared of old unto me, saying, Yea, *I have loved thee with an everlasting love:* therefore with lovingkindness have I drawn thee." Jeremiah 31:3.

Can anything separate the true child of God from the love of God?

"For I am persuaded, that neither death, nor life, nor angels, nor principalities, nor powers, nor things present, nor things to come, nor height, nor depth, nor any other creature, shall be able to separate us from the love of God, which is in Christ Jesus our Lord." Romans 8:38, 39.

Good News About
THE END OF SIN AND SUFFERING

THE FIRST SINNER

With whom did sin originate?

"He that committeth sin is of the devil; for *the devil sinneth from the beginning."* 1 John 3:8.

> NOTE—Without the Bible, the question of the origin of evil would remain unexplained.

From what time has the devil been a murderer?

"Ye are of your father the devil, and the lusts of your father ye will do. *He was a murderer from the beginning,* and abode not in the truth, because there is no truth in him." John 8:44.

What is the devil's relationship to lying?

"When he speaketh a lie, he speaketh of his own: for *he is a liar, and the father of it."* Verse 44.

Was Satan created sinful?

"Thou wast *perfect* in thy ways from the day that thou wast created, *till iniquity was found in thee."* Ezekiel 28:15.

> NOTE—Ezekiel here refers to Satan under the figure "king of Tyrus." (See verse 12.) This, and the statement in John 8:44, that he *"abode* not in the truth," show that Satan was once *perfect,* and *in the truth.* Peter speaks of "the angels that *sinned"* (2 Peter 2:4); and Jude refers to "the angels which *kept not their first estate"* (Jude 6). These angels were once in a state of sinlessness.

What further statement of Christ seems to lay the responsibility for the origin of sin upon Satan and his angels?

"Then shall he say also unto them on the left hand, Depart from me, ye cursed, into everlasting fire, *prepared for the devil and his angels."* Matthew 25:41.

SATAN AND CHRIST CONTRASTED

What led to Satan's sin, rebellion, and downfall?

"Thine heart was lifted up because of thy beauty, thou hast corrupted thy wisdom by reason of thy *brightness."* Ezekiel 28:17. "Thou hast said in thine heart, *I will ascend into heaven, I will exalt my throne above the stars of God: I will sit also upon the mount of the congregation, in the sides of the north: . . . I will be like the most High."* Isaiah 14:13, 14.

> NOTE—In a word, pride and self-exaltation led to Satan's downfall, and for these there is no justification or adequate excuse. "Pride goeth before destruction, and an haughty spirit before a fall." Proverbs 16:18. Hence, while we may know of the origin, cause, character, and results of evil, no good or sufficient reason or excuse can be given for it. To excuse it is to justify it; and the moment it is justified, it ceases to be sin. All sin is a manifestation of selfishness in some form, and its results are the opposite of those prompted by love. The experiment of sin will result finally in its utter abandonment and banishment forever, by all created intelligences, throughout the entire universe of God. Only those who foolishly and persistently cling to sin will be destroyed with it. The wicked will then be destroyed, root and branch (Malachi 4:1), and the righteous shall "shine as the brightness of the firmament," and "as the stars for ever and ever" (Daniel 12:3).

In contrast with the pride and self-exaltation exhibited by Satan, what spirit did Christ manifest?

"Who, being in the form of God, thought it not robbery to be equal with God: but *made himself of no reputation,* and took upon him the form of a *servant,* and was made in the likeness of *men:* and being found in fashion as a man, *he humbled himself,* and became obedient unto *death,* even *the death of the cross."* Philippians 2:6-8.

After man had sinned, how did God show His love and His willingness to forgive?

"For God so loved the world, that he gave his only begotten Son, that whosoever believeth in him should not perish, but have everlasting life." John 3:16.

DEFINITION AND NATURE OF SIN

What is sin declared to be?

"Whosoever committeth sin transgresseth also the law: for *sin is the transgression of the law."* 1 John 3:4.

What precedes the manifestation of sin?

"Then when *lust* hath conceived, it bringeth forth sin." James 1:15.

THE RESULTS OF SIN

What is the final result, or fruit, of sin?

"And sin, when it is finished, bringeth forth *death."*

Verse 15. "The wages of sin is *death.*" Romans 6:23.

Upon how many of the human race did death pass as the result of Adam's transgression?

"By one man sin entered into the world, and death by sin; and so *death passed upon all men,* for that all have sinned." Romans 5:12. "In Adam *all die.*" 1 Corinthians 15:22.

How were the earth itself and its vegetation affected by Adam's sin?

"Cursed is the ground for thy sake; in sorrow shalt thou eat of it all the days of thy life; *thorns also and thistles shall it bring forth to thee."* Genesis 3:17, 18.

What additional curse came as the result of the first murder?

"And the Lord said unto Cain, . . . And *now art thou cursed from the earth,* which hath opened her mouth to receive thy brother's blood from thy hand; *when thou tillest the ground, it shall not henceforth yield unto thee her strength."* Genesis 4:9-12.

What terrible judgment came in consequence of continued sin and transgression against God?

"And the Lord said, I will destroy man whom I have created from the face of the earth." "The end of all flesh is come before me; for the earth is filled with violence." "And Noah was six hundred years old when the *flood of waters* was upon the earth." "The same day were *all the fountains of the great deep broken up, and the windows of heaven were opened."* Genesis 6:7, 13; 7:6, 11.

After the Flood, what came in consequence of further apostasy from God?

"And the Lord came down to see the city and the tower, which the children of men builded. And the Lord said, Behold, the people is one, and they have all one language; and this they begin to do: and now nothing will be restrained from them, which they have imagined to do. Go to, let us go down, and there *confound their language, that they may not understand one another's speech.* So the Lord scattered them abroad from thence upon the face of all the earth: and they left off to build the city." Genesis 11:5-8.

Into what condition has sin brought the entire creation?

"For we know that the whole creation *groaneth* and *travaileth in pain together* until now." Romans 8:22.

GOD'S DELAY IN DESTROYING SIN

What explains God's apparent delay in dealing with sin?

"The Lord is not slack concerning his promise, as some men count slackness; but is *longsuffering to us-ward,* not willing that any should perish, but that all should come to repentance." 2 Peter 3:9.

What is God's attitude toward the sinner?

"For *I have no pleasure in the death of him that dieth,* saith the Lord God: wherefore turn yourselves, and live ye." Ezekiel 18:32.

Can man free himself from the dominion of sin?

"Can the Ethiopian change his skin, or the leopard his spots? *then may ye also do good, that are accustomed to do evil."* Jeremiah 13:23.

What place has the will in determining whether man shall have life?

"And the Spirit and the bride say, Come. And let him that heareth say, Come. And let him that is athirst come. And *whosoever will, let him take the water of life freely."* Revelation 22:17.

CHRIST, THE SINNER, AND SATAN

To what extent has Christ suffered for sinners?

"He was *wounded* for our transgressions, he was *bruised* for our iniquities: the *chastisement* of our peace was upon him; and with his *stripes* we are healed." Isaiah 53:5.

For what purpose was Christ manifested?

"And ye know that *he was manifested to take away our sins;* and in him is no sin. . . . He that committeth sin is of the devil; for the devil sinneth from the beginning. For this purpose the Son of God was manifested, *that he might destroy the works of the devil."* 1 John 3:5-8.

What was one direct purpose of the incarnation of Christ?

"Forasmuch then as the children are partakers of flesh and blood, he also himself likewise took part of the same; *that through death he might destroy him that had the power of death, that is, the devil."* Hebrews 2:14.

THE END OF SIN AND SORROW

What triumphant chorus will mark the end of the reign of sin?

"And every creature which is in heaven, and on the earth, and under the earth, and such as are in the sea, and all that are in them, heard I saying, *Blessing, and honour, and glory, and power, be unto him that sitteth upon the throne, and unto the Lamb for ever and ever."* Revelation 5:13.

THE END OF SIN AND SUFFERING

When and by what means will the effects of sin be removed?

"But the day of the Lord will come as a thief in the night; in the which the heavens shall pass away with a great noise, and *the elements shall melt with fervent heat, the earth also and the works that are therein shall be burned up."* 2 Peter 3:10.

How thoroughly will the effects of sin be removed?

"And God shall *wipe away all tears* from their eyes; and there shall be *no more death, neither sorrow, nor crying, neither shall there be any more pain: for the former things are passed away."* Revelation 21:4. *"And there shall be no more curse:* but the throne of God and of the Lamb shall be in it [the Holy City]; and his servants shall serve him." Revelation 22:3.

Will sin and its evil results ever appear again?

"There shall be *no more death."* "And there shall be *no more curse."* Revelation 21:4; 22:3.

GOD moves in a mysterious way
  His wonders to perform;
He plants His footsteps in the sea,
  And rides upon the storm.

Deep in unfathomable mines
  Of never-failing skill,
He treasures up His bright designs,
  And works His sovereign will.

Ye fearful saints fresh courage take;
  The clouds ye so much dread
Are big with mercy, and shall break
  In blessings on your head.

Judge not the Lord by feeble sense,
  But trust Him for His grace;
Behind a frowning providence
  He hides a smiling face.

His purpose will ripen fast,
  Unfolding every hour;
The bud may have a bitter taste,
  But sweet will be the flower.

Blind unbelief is sure to err,
  And scan His work in vain:
God is His own interpreter,
  And He will make it plain.
      — WILLIAM COWPER.

Good News About
THE MAN WHO WAS GOD

THE FATHER'S TESTIMONY

How has the Father shown that His Son is one person of the Godhead?

"But *unto the Son he saith,* Thy throne, *O God,* is for ever and ever: a sceptre of righteousness is the sceptre of thy kingdom." Hebrews 1:8.

How was He recognized by the Father while on earth?

"And lo a voice from heaven, saying, *This is my beloved Son,* in whom I am well pleased." Matthew 3:17.

CHRIST'S TESTIMONY

In what way did Christ refer to the eternity of His being?

"And now, O Father, glorify thou me with thine own self with the glory which I had with thee *before the world was.*" John 17:5. "But thou, Bethlehem Ephratah, though thou be little among the thousands of Judah, yet out of thee shall he come forth unto me that is to be ruler in Israel; whose goings forth have been of old, *from everlasting.*" Micah 5:2. (See margin, and Matthew 2:6; John 8:58; Exodus 3:13, 14.)

What does Christ say is His relation to the Father?

"I and My Father are *one.*" John 10:30.

How did Christ assert an equal proprietorship with His Father in the kingdom?

"The Son of man shall send forth his angels, and they shall gather out of *his kingdom* all things that offend, and them which do iniquity." Matthew 13:41.

To whom do the elect equally belong?

"And shall not God avenge *his own elect,* which cry day and night unto him, though he bear long with them?" Luke 18:7. "And he [the Son of man] shall send his angels with a great sound of a trumpet, and they shall gather together *his elect* from the four winds, from one end of heaven to the other." Matthew 24:31.

Who are equally joined in bestowing the final rewards?

"But without faith it is impossible to please him [God the Father]: for he that cometh to God must believe that he is, and that *he is a rewarder of them that diligently seek him.*" Hebrews 11:6. "For the Son of man shall come in the glory of his Father with his angels; and *then he shall reward every man according to his works.*" Matthew 16:27.

NOTE—In the texts (Matthew 16:27; 13:41; 24:31) in which Christ refers to the angels as "his angels" and to the kingdom as "his kingdom" and to the elect as "his elect," He refers to Himself as "the Son of man." It thus appears that while He was on earth as a man, He recognized His essential deity and His equality with His Father in heaven.

What does God declare Himself to be?

"Thus saith the Lord the King of Israel, and his redeemer the Lord of hosts; I am the *first,* and I am the *last;* and beside me there is no God." Isaiah 44:6.

In what scripture does Christ adopt the same expression?

"And, behold, I come quickly; and my reward is with me, to give every man according as his work shall be. I am Alpha and Omega, the beginning and the end, the *first* and the *last.*" Revelation 22:12, 13.

APOSTLES JOHN AND PAUL SPEAK

What scripture states that the Son of God was God manifested in the flesh?

"In the beginning was the Word, and the Word was with God, and *the Word was God.*" "And *the Word was made flesh,* and dwelt among us, (and we beheld his glory, the glory as of the only begotten of the Father,) full of grace and truth." John 1:1, 14.

What fullness dwells in Christ?

"For in him dwelleth *all the fulness of the Godhead bodily.*" Colossians 2:9.

CHRIST THE SAVIOUR

How was He manifested on earth as a Saviour?

"For unto you is *born* this day in the city of David a Saviour, which is Christ the Lord." Luke 2:11.

How was Christ begotten in the flesh?

"And the angel answered and said unto her, *The Holy Ghost* shall come upon thee, and *the power of the Highest* shall overshadow thee: therefore also that holy thing which shall be born of thee shall be called the Son of God." Luke 1:35.

Why was it necessary that He should be born thus, and partake of human nature?

"Wherefore in all things it behoved him to be made like unto his brethren, *that he might be a merciful and faithful high priest in things pertaining to God,* to make reconciliation for the sins of the people." Hebrews 2:17.

Having such a wonderful Saviour, what are we exhorted to do?

"Seeing then that we have a great high priest, that is passed into the heavens, Jesus the Son of God, *let us hold fast our profession.* For we have not an high priest which cannot be touched with the feeling of our infirmities; but was in all points tempted like as we are, yet without sin." Hebrews 4:14, 15.

Good News About

OUR FUTURE HOME

ETERNAL LIFE AND HOW TO OBTAIN IT

What precious promise has God made to His children?

"And this is the promise that he hath promised us, even *eternal life.*" 1 John 2:25.

How may we obtain eternal life?

"For God so loved the world, that he gave his only begotten Son, *that whosoever believeth in him should not perish, but have everlasting life.*" John 3:16.

Who has everlasting life?

"He that believeth on the Son hath everlasting life." Verse 36.

Where is this everlasting or eternal life?

"And this is the record, that God hath given to us eternal life, and *this life is in his Son.*" 1 John 5:11.

What therefore follows?

"He that hath the Son hath life; and he that hath not the Son of God hath not life." Verse 12.

What does Christ give His followers?

"I give unto them *eternal life;* and they shall never perish." John 10:28.

THE TREE OF LIFE, PAST AND FUTURE

Why, after the Fall, was man shut away from the tree of life?

"Lest he put forth his hand, and *take also of the tree of life, and eat, and live for ever."* Genesis 3:22.

What has Christ promised the overcomer?

"To him that overcometh will I give *to eat of the tree of life,* which is in the midst of the paradise of God." Revelation 2:7.

WHEN SAINTS BECOME IMMORTAL

When will immortality be conferred upon the saints?

"We shall not all sleep, but we shall all be changed, in a moment, in the twinkling of an eye, at the last trump: for the trumpet shall sound, and the dead shall be raised incorruptible, and we shall be changed. For this corruptible must put on incorruption, and this mortal must put on immortality." 1 Corinthians 15:51-53.

NOTE—In accepting Christ, the believer receives "that eternal life, which was with the Father," and this eternal life he retains as long as Christ dwells in the heart by faith. This wondrous gift may be lost by failure to maintain the faith which holds Christ fast. At the resurrection, immortality is conferred upon those who have fallen asleep in Christ, and thus the possession of eternal life becomes a permanent experience.

GOD'S PURPOSE IN CREATION

For what purpose was the earth created?

"For thus saith the Lord that created the heavens; God himself that formed the earth and made it; he hath established it, he created it not in vain, *he formed it to be inhabited."* Isaiah 45:18.

To whom has God given the earth?

"The heaven, even the heavens, are the Lord's: but *the earth hath he given to the children of men."* Psalm 115:16.

For what purpose was man made?

"Thou madest him *to have dominion over the works of thy hands;* thou hast put all things under his feet." Psalm 8:6. (See Genesis 1:26; Hebrews 2:8.)

SATAN, AND MAN'S LOST DOMINION

How did man lose his dominion?

Through sin. (Romans 5:12; 6:23.)

When man lost his dominion, to whom did he yield it?

"For of whom a man is overcome, of the same is he brought in bondage." 2 Peter 2:19.

NOTE—Man was overcome by Satan in the Garden of Eden, and there yielded himself and his possessions into the hands of his captor.

In tempting Christ, what ownership did Satan claim?

"And the devil, taking him up into an high mountain, shewed unto him all the kingdoms of the world in a moment of time. And the devil said unto him, All this power will I give thee, and the glory of them: *for that is delivered unto me; and to whomsoever I will I give it."* Luke 4:5, 6.

THE RESTORED DOMINION

What promise of restoration did the Lord make through Micah?

"And thou, *O tower of the flock,* the strong hold of the daughter of Zion, *unto thee shall it come, even the first dominion;* the kingdom shall come to the daughter of Jerusalem." Micah 4:8.

Why did Christ say the meek are blessed?

"Blessed are the meek: *for they shall inherit the earth."* Matthew 5:5.

NOTE—This inheritance cannot be realized in this life, for here the truly meek generally have little of earth's good things.

Who does the psalmist say have most now?

"For I was envious at *the foolish,* when I saw the prosperity of *the wicked. . . .* Their eyes stand out with fatness: *they have more than heart could wish."* Psalm 73:3-7.

What promise was made to Abraham concerning the land?

"And the Lord said unto Abram, after that Lot was separated from him, Lift up now thine eyes, and look from the place where thou art northward, and southward, and eastward, and westward: for *all the land which thou seest, to thee will I give it, and to thy SEED for ever."* Genesis 13:14, 15.

How much did this promise comprehend?

"For the promise, that he should be the heir of the world, was not to Abraham, or to his seed, through the law, but through the righteousness of faith." Romans 4:13.

How much of the land of Canaan did Abraham own in his lifetime?

"And he gave him none inheritance in it, no, not so much as to set his foot on: yet he promised that he would give it to him for a possession, and to his seed after him, when as yet he had no child." Acts 7:5. (See Hebrews 11:13.)

How much of the promised possession did Abraham expect during his lifetime?

"By faith Abraham, when he was called to go out into a place which he should after receive for an inheritance, obeyed; and he went out, not knowing whither he went. By faith *he sojourned in the land of promise, as in a strange country,* dwelling in tabernacles with Isaac and Jacob, the heirs with him of the same promise: *for he looked for a city which hath foundations, whose builder and maker is God."* Hebrews 11:8-10.

Who is the seed to whom this promise was made?

"Now to Abraham and his seed were the promises made. He saith not, And to seeds, as of many; but as of one, *And to thy seed, which is Christ."* Galatians 3:16.

Who are heirs of the promise?

"And *if ye be Christ's, then are ye Abraham's seed, and heirs according to the promise."* Verse 29.

Why did not these ancient worthies receive the promise?

"And these all, having obtained a good report through faith, received not the promise: God having provided some better thing for us, *that they without us should not be made perfect."* Hebrews 11:39, 40.

WHEN THIS EARTH IS MADE NEW

What is to become of our earth in the day of the Lord?

"But the day of the Lord will come as a thief in the night; in the which the heavens shall pass away with a great noise, and *the elements shall melt with fervent heat, the earth also and the works that are therein shall be burned up."* 2 Peter 3:10.

What will follow this great conflagration?

"Nevertheless we, according to his promise, *look for new heavens and a new earth,* wherein dwelleth righteousness." Verse 13.

NOTE—As shown in the reading on "The Millennium," at the coming of Christ the living wicked will die, and the saints will be taken to heaven to dwell with Christ a thousand years, or until the wicked of all ages are judged and the time comes for their destruction and the purification of the earth by the fires of the last day. Following this, the earth will be formed anew, and man, redeemed from sin, will be restored to his original dominion.

To what Old Testament promise did Peter evidently refer?

"For, behold, I create new heavens and a new earth: and the former shall not be remembered, nor come into mind." Isaiah 65:17.

What was shown the apostle John in vision?

"And I saw *a new heaven and a new earth:* for the first heaven and the first earth were passed away; and there was no more sea." Revelation 21:1.

How did Isaiah describe conditions on the "new earth"?

"And they shall build houses, and inhabit them; and they shall plant vineyards, and eat the fruit of them. They shall not build, and another inhabit; they shall not plant, and another eat: for as the days of a tree are the days of my people, and mine elect shall long enjoy the work of their hands. They shall not labour in vain, nor bring forth for trouble; for they are the seed of the blessed of the Lord, and their offspring with them." Isaiah 65:21-23.

How readily will their wants be supplied?

"And it shall come to pass, that before they call, I will answer; and while they are yet speaking, I will hear." Verse 24.

What peaceful condition will reign throughout the earth then?

"The wolf and the lamb shall feed together, and the lion shall eat straw like the bullock: and dust shall be the serpent's meat. They shall not hurt nor destroy in all my holy mountain, saith the Lord." Verse 25.

What seasons of worship will be observed in the new earth?

"For as the new heavens and the new earth, which I will make, shall remain before me, saith the Lord, so shall your seed and your name remain. And it shall come to pass, that *from one new moon to another, and from one sabbath to another,* shall all flesh come to worship before me, saith the Lord." Isaiah 66:22, 23.

What will the ransomed of the Lord then do?

"And the ransomed of the Lord shall return, and come to Zion with songs and everlasting joy upon their heads: they shall obtain joy and gladness, and sorrow and sighing shall flee away." Isaiah 35:10.

A REAL CITY

What was one of Christ's parting promises to His disciples?

"In my Father's house are many mansions: if it were not so, I would have told you. *I go to prepare a place for you.*" John 14:2.

What does Paul say God has prepared for His people?

"But now they desire a better country, that is, an heavenly: wherefore God is not ashamed to be called their God: for *he hath prepared for them a city.*" Hebrews 11:16.

Where is this city, and what is it called?

"But *Jerusalem which is above* is free, which is the mother of us all." Galatians 4:26.

For what did Abraham look?

"For *he looked for a city* which hath foundations, whose builder and maker is God." Hebrews 11:10.

What assurance has God given to believers?

"God is not ashamed to be called their God: for he hath prepared for them a city." Hebrews 11:16.

SAINT JOHN DESCRIBES THE CITY

What did John see concerning this city?

"And *I John saw the holy city, new Jerusalem, coming down from God out of heaven,* prepared as a bride adorned for her husband." Revelation 21:2.

How many foundations has this city?

"And the wall of the city had *twelve foundations,* and in them the names of the twelve apostles of the Lamb." Verse 14.

What is the measurement of the city?

"And the city lieth foursquare, and the length is as large as the breadth: and *he measured the city with the reed, twelve thousand furlongs."* Verse 16.

What is the height of the wall?

"And he measured the wall thereof, *an hundred and forty and four cubits."* Verse 17.

NOTE—One hundred and forty-four cubits are estimated at 216 feet in our measure.

Of what material is the wall constructed?

"And the building of *the wall of it was of jasper:* and the city was pure gold, like unto clear glass." Verse 18.

With what are the twelve foundations adorned?

"And the foundations of the wall of the city were garnished with all manner of precious stones. The first foundation was *jasper;* the second, *sapphire;* the third, a *chalcedony;* the fourth, an *emerald;* the fifth, *sardonyx;* the sixth, *sardius;* the seventh, *chrysolyte;* the eighth, *beryl;* the ninth, a *topaz;* the tenth, a *chrysoprasus;* the eleventh, a *jacinth;* the twelfth, an *amethyst."* Verses 19, 20. (See Exodus 28:15-21; Isaiah 54:11, 12.)

Of what are the twelve gates composed?

"And the twelve gates were *twelve pearls:* every several gate was of one pearl." Revelation 21:21.

What is written on these gates?

"The names of the twelve tribes of the children of Israel." Verse 12.

The Reward of the Saved
Harry Anderson, Artist

Of what does John say the streets of the city are composed?

"And the street of the city was *pure gold, as it were transparent glass.*" Verse 21.

Why will this city have no need of the sun or moon?

"And the city had no need of the sun, neither of the moon, to shine in it: *for the glory of God did lighten it, and the Lamb is the light thereof. And the nations of them which are saved shall walk in the light of it: and the kings of the earth do bring their glory and honour into it.*" Verses 23, 24. (See Revelation 22:5; Isaiah 60:19, 20.)

Why are its gates not to be closed?

"And the gates of it shall not be shut at all by day: *for there shall be no night there.*" Revelation 21:25.

WHO MAY, AND WHO MAY NOT, ENTER

What will be excluded from this city?

"And there shall in no wise enter into it *any thing that defileth, neither whatsoever worketh abomination, or maketh a lie.*" Verse 27.

Who will be permitted to enter it?

"*Blessed are they that do his commandments,* that they may have right to the tree of life, and may enter in through the gates into the city." Revelation 22:14.

NOTE—The late English and American revisions render this, "Blessed are they that wash their robes," etc. The result is the same, for those who wash their robes cease to sin, and hence do God's commandments.

When this city becomes the metropolis of the new earth, what will be the condition of God's people?

"And God shall wipe away all tears from their eyes; and there shall be no more death, neither sorrow, nor crying, neither shall there be any more pain: for the former things are passed away." Revelation 21:4.

EVERLASTING LIFE AND GLORIOUS PRIVILEGE

What will flow through the city?

"And he shewed me *a pure river of water of life,* clear as crystal, proceeding out of the throne of God and of the Lamb." Revelation 22:1.

What stands on either side of the river?

"In the midst of the street of it, and on either side of the river, was there *the tree of life,* which bare twelve manner of fruits, and yielded her fruit every month: and the leaves of the tree were for the healing of the nations." Verse 2.

NOTE—The tree of life, which Adam lost through transgression, is to be restored by Christ. Access to this is one of the promises to the overcomer. (Revelation 2:7.) Its bearing 12 kinds of fruit, a new kind each month, suggests a reason why in the new earth "from one *new moon* to another," as well as "from one sabbath to another," all flesh is to come before God to worship, as stated in Isaiah 66:22, 23.

CHRIST THE WAY OF LIFE

What does Jesus declare Himself to be?

"Jesus saith unto him, *I am the way, the truth, and the life:* no man cometh unto the Father, but by me." John 14:6.

MAN'S SITUATION

In what condition are all men?

"But the scripture hath concluded all *under sin.*" Galatians 3:22. "For *all have sinned,* and come short of the glory of God." Romans 3:23.

What are the wages of sin?

"The wages of sin is *death.*" Romans 6:23.

How many are affected by Adam's transgression?

"Wherefore, as by one man sin entered into the world, and death by sin; and so *death passed upon all men.*" Romans 5:12.

When man first transgressed, what was done to prevent him from living forever in sin?

"And now, lest he put forth his hand, and take also of the tree of life, and eat, and live for ever. . . . *So he drove out the man;* and he placed at the east of the garden of Eden Cherubims, and a flaming sword which turned every way, to keep the way of the tree of life." Genesis 3:22-24.

GOD'S GIFT AND REMEDY

What is the gift of God?

"The gift of God is *eternal life.*" Romans 6:23.

How many may receive this gift?

"And the Spirit and the bride say, Come. And let him that heareth say, Come. And let him that is athirst come. And *whosoever will,* let him take the water of life freely." Revelation 22:17.

In whom is the gift?

"This is the record, that God hath given to us eternal life, and *this life is in his Son.*" 1 John 5:11.

In receiving the Son, what do we have in Him?

"He that hath the Son hath *life.*" Verse 12.

What loss do those sustain who do not accept Him?

"And he that hath not the Son of God *hath not life.*" Verse 12.

In what other way is this same truth stated?

"He that believeth on the Son hath everlasting life: and he that believeth not the Son shall not see life; but the wrath of God abideth on him." John 3:36.

After one truly receives Christ, whose life will be manifested in him?

"I am crucified with Christ: nevertheless I live; yet not I, but *Christ liveth in me:* and the life which I now live in the flesh I live by the faith of the Son of God, who loved me, and gave himself for me." Galatians 2:20.

SPIRITUAL DEATH AND REBIRTH

In what condition are all before they are quickened with Christ?

"God, who is rich in mercy, for his great love wherewith he loved us, even when we were *dead in sins,* hath quickened us together with Christ." Ephesians 2:4, 5.

What is this change from death to life called?

"Being *born again,* not of corruptible seed, but of incorruptible, by the word of God, which liveth and abideth for ever." 1 Peter 1:23.

SALVATION THROUGH FAITH

What is declared to be one purpose of Christ's death?

"Forasmuch then as the children are partakers of flesh and blood, he also himself likewise took part of the same; *that through death he might destroy him that had the power of death, that is, the devil."* Hebrews 2:14.

Why have all been reckoned under sin?

"But the scripture hath concluded all under sin, *that the promise by faith of Jesus Christ might be given to them that believe."* Galatians 3:22.

How then do all become children of God?

"For ye are all the children of God *by faith in Christ Jesus."* Verse 26.

With whom are the children of God joint heirs?

"If children, then heirs; heirs of God, and *joint-heirs with Christ."* Romans 8:17.

Good News About
SALVATION

SIN AND REPENTANCE

Who are called to repentance?

"I came not to call the righteous, but *sinners* to repentance." Luke 5:32.

What accompanies repentance?

"And that repentance and *remission of sins* should be preached in his name among all nations." Luke 24:47.

By what means is it made known?

"By the law is the knowledge of sin." Romans 3:20.

How many are sinners?

"We have before proved *both Jews and Gentiles,* that *they are all under sin."* Verse 9.

What do transgressors bring upon themselves?

"Let no man deceive you with vain words: for because of these things cometh *the wrath of God* upon the children of disobedience." Ephesians 5:6.

EXPERIENCING SALVATION

Who awakens the soul to a sense of its sinful condition?

"When he *[the Comforter] is come, he will reprove* [literally, *"convince"] the world of sin."* John 16:8.

What are fitting inquiries for those convicted?

"Men and brethren, *what shall we do?"* "Sirs, *what must I do to be saved?"* Acts 2:37; 16:30.

What replies does Inspiration return to these inquiries?

"Repent, and be baptized every one of you in the name of Jesus Christ for the remission of sins." *"Believe on the Lord Jesus Christ,* and thou shalt be saved." Acts 2:38; 16:31.

FRUITS OF TRUE REPENTANCE

What will the truly repentant sinner be constrained to do?

"I will *declare mine iniquity;* I will be *sorry* for my sin." Psalm 38:18.

What is the result of godly sorrow?

"For godly sorrow *worketh repentance to salvation."* 2 Corinthians 7:10.

What does the sorrow of the world do?

"The sorrow of the world *worketh death."* Verse 10.

How does godly sorrow for sin manifest itself?

"For behold this selfsame thing, that ye sorrowed after a godly sort, what *carefulness* it wrought in you, yea, what *clearing of yourselves,* yea, what indignation, yea, what fear, yea, what vehement desire, yea, what zeal, yea, what revenge! In all things ye have approved yourselves to be clear in this matter." Verse 11.

What did John the Baptist say to the Pharisees and Sadducees when he saw them come to his baptism?

"O generation of vipers, who hath warned you to flee from the wrath to come?" Matthew 3:7.

What did he tell them to do?

"Bring forth therefore fruits meet for repentance." Verse 8.

> NOTE—There can be no true repentance without reformation. Repentance is a change of mind; reformation is a corresponding change of life.

When God sent the Ninevites a warning message, how did they show their repentance, and what was the result?

"And God saw their works, that *they turned from their evil way; and God repented of the evil, that he had said that he would do unto them; and he did it not."* Jonah 3:10.

What leads sinners to repentance?

"Or despisest thou the riches of his goodness and forbearance and longsuffering; not knowing that *the goodness of God leadeth thee to repentance?"* Romans 2:4.

Salvation Through Faith

Harry Anderson, Artist

CONFESSION AND FORGIVENESS

What instruction is given concerning confession of sin?

"Speak unto the children of Israel, When a man or woman shall commit any sin that men commit, to do a trespass against the Lord, and that person be guilty; *then they shall confess their sin which they have done."* Numbers 5:6, 7.

How futile is it to attempt to hide sin from God?

"But if ye will not do so, behold, ye have sinned against the Lord: and *be sure your sin will find you out."* Numbers 32:23. "Thou hast set our iniquities before thee, our secret sins in the light of thy countenance." Psalm 90:8. "All things are naked and opened unto the eyes of him with whom we have to do." Hebrews 4:13.

What promise is made to those who confess their sins?

"If we confess our sins, *he is faithful and just to forgive us our sins,* and to cleanse us from all unrighteousness." 1 John 1:9.

What different results attend the covering and the confessing of sins?

"He that covereth his sins *shall not prosper:* but whoso confesseth and forsaketh them *shall have mercy."* Proverbs 28:13.

BEING DEFINITE IN CONFESSION

How definite should we be in confessing our sins?

"And it shall be, when he shall be guilty in one of these things, that he shall confess that he hath sinned *in that thing."* Leviticus 5:5.

> NOTE—"True confession is always of a specific character, and acknowledges particular sins. They may be of such a nature as to be brought before God only; they may be wrongs that should be confessed to individuals who have suffered injury through them; or they may be of a public character, and should then be as publicly confessed. But all confession should be definite and to the point, acknowledging the very sins of which you are guilty."—*Steps to Christ,* p. 43.

How fully did Israel once acknowledge their wrongdoing?

"And all the people said unto Samuel, Pray for thy servants unto the Lord thy God, that we die not: for *we have added unto all our sins this evil, to ask us a king."* 1 Samuel 12:19.

When David confessed his sin, what did he say God did?

"I acknowledged my sin unto thee, and mine iniquity have I not hid. I said, I will confess my trans-gressions unto the Lord; and *thou forgavest the iniquity of my sin."* Psalm 32:5.

GOD'S DELIGHT IN FORGIVING

What is God ready to do for all who seek for forgiveness?

"For thou, Lord, art good, and *ready to forgive;* and plenteous in mercy unto all them that call upon thee." Psalm 86:5.

Upon what did David rest his hope of forgiveness?

"Have mercy upon me, O God, *according to thy lovingkindness: according unto the multitude of thy tender mercies* blot out my transgressions." Psalm 51:1.

What is the measure of the greatness of God's mercy?

"For *as the heaven is high above the earth,* so great is his mercy toward them that fear him." Psalm 103:11.

How fully does the Lord pardon when one repents?

"Let the wicked forsake his way, and the unrighteous man his thoughts: and let him return unto the Lord, and he will have mercy upon him; and to our God, for *he will abundantly pardon."* Isaiah 55:7.

What reason is given for God's readiness to forgive sin?

"Who is a God like unto thee, that pardoneth iniquity, and passeth by the transgression of the remnant of his heritage? He retaineth not his anger for ever, *because he delighteth in mercy."* Micah 7:18. (See Psalm 78:38.)

Why does God manifest such mercy and longsuffering toward men who seem to be holding on to sin?

"The Lord is not slack concerning his promise, as some men count slackness; but is longsuffering to us-ward, *not willing that any should perish,* but that all should come to repentance." 2 Peter 3:9.

SPECIFIC EXAMPLES

When the prodigal son, in the parable, repented and turned toward home, what did his father do?

"When he was yet a great way off, his father saw him, and *had compassion,* and ran, and fell on his neck, and kissed him." Luke 15:20.

How did the father show his joy at his son's return?

"The father said to his servants, *Bring forth the best robe, and put it on him;* and put a ring on his hand, and shoes on his feet: and *bring hither the fat-*

ted calf, and kill it; and let us eat, and be merry: for this my son was dead, and is alive again; he was lost, and is found." Verses 22-24.

What is felt in heaven when a sinner repents?

"Likewise, I say unto you, *there is joy in the presence of the angels of God* over one sinner that repenteth." Verse 10.

What did Hezekiah say God had done with his sins?

"Behold, for peace I had great bitterness: but thou hast in love to my soul delivered it from the pit of corruption: *for thou hast cast all my sins behind thy back."* Isaiah 38:17.

How completely does God wish to separate sin from us?

"Thou wilt cast all their sins into the depths of the sea." Micah 7:19. "As far as the east is from the west, so far hath he removed our transgressions from us." Psalm 103:12.

How did the people respond to the preaching of John?

"Then went out to him Jerusalem, and all Judea, and all the region round about Jordan, and were baptized of him in Jordan, *confessing their sins."* Matthew 3:5, 6.

How did some of the believers at Ephesus testify to the sincerity of the confession of their sins?

"And many that believed came, and *confessed, and shewed their deeds.* Many of them also which used curious arts *brought their books together, and burned them before all men:* and they counted the price of them, and found it fifty thousand pieces of silver." Acts 19:18, 19.

CONDITIONS OF FORGIVENESS

Upon what basis has Christ taught us to ask forgiveness?

"And forgive us our debts, *as we forgive our debtors."* Matthew 6:12.

What spirit must those cherish whom God forgives?

"For *if ye forgive men their trespasses,* your heavenly Father will also forgive you: but if ye forgive not men their trespasses, neither will your Father forgive your trespasses." Verses 14, 15.

What exhortation is based on the fact that God has forgiven us?

"And be ye kind one to another, tenderhearted, *forgiving one another,* even as God for Christ's sake hath forgiven you." Ephesians 4:32.

THE BLESSED GIVER AND RECEIVER

Through whom are repentance and forgiveness granted?

"The God of our fathers raised up *Jesus,* whom ye slew and hanged on a tree. him hath God exalted with his right hand to be a Prince and a Saviour, for *to give repentance* to Israel, and *forgiveness of sins."* Acts 5:30, 31.

In what condition is one whose sins are forgiven?

"Blessed is he whose transgression is forgiven, whose sin is covered. Blessed is the man unto whom the Lord imputeth not iniquity, and in whose spirit there is no guile." Psalm 32:1, 2.

Good News About
LIVING FOR CHRIST

NECESSITY OF CONVERSION

How did Jesus emphasize the necessity of conversion?

"Verily I say unto you, *Except ye be converted,* and become as little children, *ye shall not enter into the kingdom of heaven."* Matthew 18:3.

In what other statement did He teach the same truth?

"Verily, verily, I say unto thee, *Except a man be born again,* he cannot see the kingdom of God." John 3:3.

How did He further explain the new birth?

"Jesus answered, Verily, verily, I say unto thee, *Except a man be born of water and of the Spirit,* he cannot enter into the kingdom of God." Verse 5.

With what comparison did He illustrate the subject?

"The wind bloweth where it listeth, and thou hearest the sound thereof, but canst not tell whence it cometh, and whither it goeth: *so is every one that is born of the Spirit."* Verse 8.

AGENCY OF THE NEW CREATION

What takes place when one is converted to Christ?

"Wherefore if any man is in Christ, *he is a new creation:* the old things are passed away; behold, they are become new." 2 Corinthians 5:17, RV, margin. (See Acts 9:1-22; 22:1-21; 26:1-23.)

What is the value of merely outward forms?

"For in Christ Jesus *neither circumcision availeth any thing, nor uncircumcision,* but a new creature." Galatians 6:15.

Through what was the original creation wrought?

"By the word of the Lord were the heavens made; and all the host of them by the breath of his mouth." Psalm 33:6.

Through what instrumentality is conversion wrought?

"Being born again, not of corruptible seed, but of incorruptible, *by the word of God,* which liveth and abideth for ever." 1 Peter 1:23.

RESULTS OF TRUE CONVERSION

What change is wrought in conversion, or the new birth?

"Even when we were dead in sins, hath *quickened* us together with Christ, (by grace ye are saved)." Ephesians 2:5.

What is one evidence of this change from death to life?

"We know that we have passed from death unto life, because *we love the brethren.* he that loveth not his brother abideth in death." 1 John 3:14.

From what is a converted sinner saved?

"Let him know, that he which converteth the sinner from the error of his way, shall save a soul from *death,* and shall hide a multitude of sins." James 5:20. (See Acts 26:14-18.)

To whom are sinners brought by conversion?

"Create in me a clean heart, O God; and renew a right spirit within me. . . . Then will I teach transgressors thy ways; and sinners shall be *converted unto thee."* Psalm 51:10-13.

In what words to Peter did Jesus indicate the kind of service a converted person should render to his brethren?

"And the Lord said, Simon, Simon, behold, Satan hath desired to have you, that he may sift you as wheat: but I have prayed for thee, that thy faith fail not: and *when thou art converted, strengthen thy brethren."* Luke 22:31, 32.

What other experience is associated with conversion?

"For this people's heart is waxed gross, and their ears are dull of hearing, and their eyes they have closed; lest at any time they should see with their eyes, and hear with their ears, and should understand with their heart, and should be *converted,* and I should *heal them."* Matthew 13:15.

What gracious promise does God make to His people?

"I will heal their backsliding, I will love them freely: for mine anger is turned away from him." Hosea 14:4.

By what means is this healing accomplished?

"He [Christ] was wounded for our transgressions, he was bruised for our iniquities: the chastisement of our peace was upon him; and *with his stripes we are healed."* Isaiah 53:5.

What are the evidences that one has been born of God?

"If ye know that he is righteous, ye know that *every one that doeth righteousness is born of him."* "Beloved, let us love one another: for love is of God; and *every one that loveth is born of God,* and knoweth God." 1 John 2:29; 4:7.

What indwelling power keeps such from sinning?

"Whosoever is born of God doth not commit sin; for *his* [God's] *seed remaineth in him:* and he cannot sin, because he is born of God." 1 John 3:9. (See 1 John 5:4; Genesis 39:9.)

What will be the experience of those born of the Spirit?

"There is therefore now *no condemnation* to them which are in Christ Jesus, who walk not after the flesh, but after the Spirit." Romans 8:1.

BELIEVING AND BEHOLDING JESUS

What is true of everyone who believes in Jesus?

"Whosoever believeth that Jesus is the Christ is *born of God."* 1 John 5:1.

What change is wrought by beholding Jesus?

"But we all, with open face beholding as in a glass the glory of the Lord, are *changed into the same image* from glory to glory even as by the Spirit of the Lord." 2 Corinthians 3:18.

NOTE—We were slaves to sin. Jesus came down and suffered with us, and for us and delivered us. As we behold Him in His Word and in prayer and meditation, and serve Him in the person of others, we may be changed more and more into the glory of His likeness; then, if faithful, we shall someday see Him "face to face."

Good News About
THE END
OF THE WORLD

JERUSALEM'S DESTRUCTION AND ITS MEANING

How did Christ feel concerning Jerusalem?

"And when he was come near, he beheld the city, and *wept over it,* saying, If thou hadst known, even thou, at least in this thy day, the things which belong unto thy peace! but now they are hid from thine eyes." Luke 19:41, 42.

In what words did He foretell its destruction?

"Thine enemies shall cast a trench about thee, and compass thee round, and keep thee in on every side, and shall lay thee even with the ground, and thy children within thee; and they shall not leave in thee one stone upon another; because thou knewest not the time of thy visitation." Verses 43, 44.

What pitiful appeal did He make to the impenitent city?

"O Jerusalem, Jerusalem, thou that killest the prophets, and stonest them which are sent unto thee, how often would I have gathered thy children together, even as a hen gathereth her chickens under her wings, and ye would not!" Matthew 23:37.

As He was about to leave the Temple, what did He say?

"Behold, your house is left unto you *desolate."* Verse 38.

NOTE—The Jews filled up their cup of iniquity by their final rejection and crucifixion of Christ, and their persecution of His followers after His resurrection. (See Matthew 23:29-35; John 19:15; Acts 4-8.)

Hearing these words, what questions did the disciples ask?

"Tell us, when shall these things be? and what shall be the sign of thy coming, and of the end of the world?" Matthew 24:3.

NOTE—The overthrow of Jerusalem and of the Jewish nation is a type of the final destruction of all the cities of the world, and of all nations. The descriptions of the two events seem to be blended. Christ's prophetic words reached beyond Jerusalem's destruction to the final conflagration; they were spoken not for the early disciples only, but for those who were to live during the closing scenes of the world's history. Christ gave defi-

nite signs, both of the destruction of Jerusalem and of His second coming.

Did Christ indicate that either event was imminent?

"Jesus answered and said unto them, *Take heed that no man deceive you.* For many shall come in my name, saying, I am Christ; and shall deceive many. And ye shall hear of wars and rumours of wars: see that ye be not troubled: *for all these things must come to pass, but the end is not yet."* Verses 4-6.

What did He say of the wars, famines, pestilences, and earthquakes that were to precede these events?

"All these are *the beginning of sorrows."* Verse 8.

NOTE—These were to precede and culminate in the overthrow, first, of Jerusalem, and finally of the whole world; for, as already noted, the prophecy has a double application, first, to Jerusalem and the Jewish nation, and second, to the whole world; the destruction of Jerusalem for its rejection of Christ at His first coming being a type of the destruction of the world at the end for its rejection of Christ in refusing to heed the closing warning message sent by God to prepare the world for Christ's second advent.

What would be the experiences of His people?

"Then shall they deliver you up to be afflicted, and shall kill you: and ye shall be hated of all nations for my name's sake. And then shall many be offended, and shall betray one another, and shall hate one another. And many false prophets shall rise, and shall deceive many. And because iniquity shall abound, the love of many shall wax cold." Verses 9-12.

Who did He say would be saved?

"But *he that shall endure unto the end,* the same shall be saved." Verse 13.

When did Christ say the end would come?

"And *this gospel of the kingdom shall be preached in all the world for a witness unto all nations; and then shall the end come."* Verse 14.

NOTE—Before the fall of Jerusalem, Paul carried the gospel to Rome—then the capital of the world. he wrote of the saints of "Caesar's household" (Philippians 4:22), and further said that the gospel had been "preached to every creature which is under heaven." Colossians 1:23.

Thus it was respecting the end of the Jewish nation; and

thus it will be in the end of the world as a whole. When the gospel, or good news, of Christ's coming kingdom has been preached in all the world for a witness unto all nations, then the end will come. As the end of the Jewish nation came with overwhelming destruction, so will come the end of the world.

What would be a sign of the fall of Jerusalem?

"And *when ye shall see Jerusalem compassed with armies,* then know that the desolation thereof is nigh." Luke 21:20.

At this time what were the disciples to do?

"When ye therefore shall see the abomination of desolation, spoken of by Daniel the prophet, stand in the holy place, (whoso readeth, let him understand:) then let them which be in Judea *flee into the mountains.*" Matthew 24:15, 16.

NOTE—In A.D. 66, when Cestius came against the city, but unaccountably withdrew, the Christians discerned in this the sign foretold by Christ, and fled (Eusebius, *Church History,* book 3, chap. 5), while 1,100,000 Jews are said to have been killed in the terrible siege in A.D. 70. Here is a striking lesson on the importance of studying the prophecies and heeding the signs of the times. Those who believed Christ and watched for the sign which He had foretold were saved, while the unbelieving perished. So in the end of the world the watchful and believing will be delivered, while the careless and unbelieving will be snared and taken. (See Matthew 24:36-44; Luke 21:34-36; 1 Thessalonians 5:1-6.)

When the sign appeared, how suddenly were they to flee?

"Let him which is on the housetop not come down to take any thing out of his house: neither let him which is in the field return back to take his clothes." Matthew 24:17, 18.

How did Christ further show His care for His disciples?

"But pray ye that your flight be not in *the winter,* neither on *the sabbath day.*" Verse 20.

NOTE—Flight in winter would entail discomfort and hardship; an attempt to flee on the Sabbath would doubtless meet with difficulty. The prayers of Christ's followers were heard. Events were so overruled that neither Jews nor Romans hindered their flight. When Cestius retreated, the Jews pursued his army, and the Christians thus had an opportunity to leave the city. The country was cleared of enemies, for at the time of this siege, the Jews had assembled at Jerusalem for the Feast of Tabernacles. Thus the Christians of Judea were able to escape unmolested, and in the autumn, a most favorable time for flight.

What trying experience did Christ then foretell?

"For *then shall be great tribulation,* such as was not since the beginning of the world to this time, no, nor ever shall be." Verse 21.

NOTE—In the siege of Jerusalem a prophecy of Moses (Deuteronomy 28:47-53) was literally fulfilled: "Thou shalt eat the fruit of thine own body, the flesh of thy sons and of

thy daughters, . . . in the siege, and in the straitness, wherewith thine enemies shall distress thee." For the fulfillment, see Josephus, *Wars of the Jews,* book 6, chap. 3, par. 4.

Following the destruction of Jerusalem came the persecution of the Christians under pagan emperors during the first three centuries of the Christian Era. Later came the greater and more terrible persecution during the long centuries of papal supremacy, foretold in Daniel 7:25 and Revelation 12:6. All these tribulations occurred under either pagan or papal Rome.

For whose sake would the period be shortened?

"And except those days should be shortened, there should no flesh be saved: but *for the elect's sake those days shall be shortened.*" Matthew 24:22.

NOTE—Through the influence of the Reformation of the sixteenth century, and the movements which grew out of it, the power of the papacy to enforce its decrees against those it pronounced heretics was gradually lessened, until persecution ceased almost wholly by the middle of the eighteenth century, before the 1260 years ended.

Against what deceptions did Christ then warn us?

"Then if any man shall say unto you, Lo, here is Christ, or there; believe it not. For there shall arise false Christs, and false prophets, and shall shew great signs and wonders; insomuch that, if it were possible, they shall deceive the very elect." Verses 23, 24.

SIGNS IN SUN, MOON, AND STARS

What signs of the end would be seen in the heavens?

"There shall be signs in the sun, and in the *moon,* and in the *stars."* Luke 21:25.

When were the first of these signs to appear?

"Immediately after the tribulation of those days shall the sun be darkened, and the moon shall not give her light, and the stars shall fall from heaven." Matthew 24:29. "But *in those days, after that tribulation,* the sun shall be darkened, and the moon shall not give her light, and the stars of heaven shall fall, and the powers that are in heaven shall be shaken." Mark 13:24, 25. Compare Joel 2:30, 31; 3:15; Isaiah 13:10; Amos 8:9.

NOTE—Within the 1260 years, but after the persecution (about the middle of the eighteenth century), the signs of His coming began to appear.

1. A *wonderful darkening of the sun and moon.* The remarkable Dark Day of May 19, 1780, is described by Samuel Williams of Harvard. The professor relates that the obscuration approached with the clouds from the southwest "between the hours of ten and eleven A.M., and continued until the middle of the next night," varying in degree and duration in different localities. In some places "persons could not see to read common print in the open air, for several hours," although "this was not generally the case."

"Candles were lighted up in the houses;—the birds having sung their evening songs, disappeared, and became silent;—the fowls retired to roost;—the cocks were crowing all around, as at break of day;—objects could not be distinguished but at a very little distance; and everything bore the appearance and gloom of night." (See *Memoirs of the American Academy of Arts and Sciences* [through 1783], vol. 1, pp. 234, 235.)

Since the moon, full the night before, was on the opposite side of the earth, there was no eclipse of the sun—nor could an eclipse last so long. The causes assigned seem inadequate to account for the area covered.

"The darkness *of the following evening* was probably as gross as ever has been observed since the Almighty fiat gave birth to light. It wanted only palpability to render it as extraordinary, as that which overspread the land of Egypt in the days of Moses. . . . If every luminous body in the universe had been shrouded in impenetrable shades, or struck out of existence, the darkness could not have been more complete. A sheet of white paper held within a few inches of the eyes was equally invisible with the blackest velvet."—SAMUEL TENNEY, Letter (1785), in *Collections of the Massachusetts Historical Society,* part 1, vol. 1 (1792 ed.), pp. 97, 98.

Timothy Dwight, president of Yale, remembered that "a very general opinion prevailed, that the day of judgment was at hand. The [Connecticut] House of Representatives, being unable to transact their business, adjourned," but the Council lighted candles, preferring, as a member said, to be found at work if the judgment were approaching. (See John W. Barber, *Connecticut Historical Collections* [2nd ed., 1836], p. 403.)

There was no agreement among the current writers as to the cause of this unparalleled darkness, but there was entire agreement as to the extraordinary character of it. Any suggestion of a natural cause or causes for the darkness can in no wise militate against the significance of the event. Sixteen and a half centuries before it occurred the Saviour had definitely foretold this twofold sign, saying, "In those days, after that tribulation, the sun shall be darkened, and the moon shall not give her light." Mark 13:24. These signs occurred exactly as predicted, and at the time indicated so long before their occurrence. It is this fact, and not the cause of the darkness, that is significant in this connection. When the Lord would open a path for his people through the sea, he did it by "a strong east wind." Exodus 14:21. Was it for this reason any less miraculous? When the bitter waters were made sweet (Exodus 15:23-25), was the divine interposition any less real because certain natural means were used, having apparently some part, under divine direction, in rendering the water fit for drinking? In like manner, even though it were possible for science to account for the remarkable darkness of May 19, 1780, instead of merely speculating concerning it, the event would not be discredited thereby as a merciful sign of the approaching end of probationary time.

2. *Remarkable display of falling stars.* "The morning of November 13th, 1833," says an eyewitness, a Yale astronomer, "was rendered memorable by an exhibition of the phenomenon called shooting stars, which was probably more extensive and magnificent than any similar one hitherto recorded. . . . Probably no celestial phenomenon has ever occurred in this country, since its first settlement, which was viewed with so much admiration and delight by one class of spectators, or with so much astonishment and fear by another class."—DENISON OLMSTED, in *The American Journal of Science and Arts,* vol. 25 (1834), pp. 363, 364.

"From the Gulf of Mexico to Halifax, until daylight with some difficulty put an end to the display, the sky was scored in every direction with shining tracks and illuminated with majestic fireballs. At Boston, the frequency of meteors was estimated to be about half that of flakes of snow in an average snowstorm. . . . Traced backwards, their paths were invariably found to converge to a point in the constellation Leo."—AGNES M. CLERKE, *A Popular History of Astronomy* (1885 ed.), pp. 369, 370.

Frederick Douglass, in reminiscing about his early days in slavery, says: "I witnessed this gorgeous spectacle, and was awe-struck. The air seemed filled with bright descending messengers from the sky. . . . I was not without the suggestion at the moment that it might be *the harbinger of the coming of the Son of Man;* and in my then state of mind I was prepared to hail Him as my friend and deliverer. I had read that 'the stars shall fall from heaven,' and they were now falling."—*Life and Times of Frederick Douglass* (1941 ed.), p. 117.

WORLD CONDITIONS, PREPARATION

What were to be the signs on earth of Christ's coming?

"Distress of nations, with perplexity; *the sea and the waves roaring; men's hearts failing them for fear,* and for looking after those things which are coming on the earth." Luke 21:25, 26.

What was to be the next great event?

"And then shall they see *the Son of man coming in a cloud with power and great glory."* Verse 27. (See Matthew 24:30.)

When these things begin to happen, what should we do?

"And when these things begin to come to pass, then *look up, and lift up your heads;* for your redemption draweth nigh." Luke 21:28.

When the trees put forth their leaves, what do we know?

"Now learn a parable of the fig tree; When his branch is yet tender, and putteth forth leaves, *ye know that summer is nigh."* Matthew 24:32.

What do we likewise know after these signs are seen?

"So likewise ye, when ye shall see all these things, *know that it is near, even at the doors."* Verse 33. "So likewise ye, when ye see these things come to pass, *know ye that the kingdom of God is nigh at hand."* Luke 21:31.

What did Christ say of the certainty of this prophecy?

35

"Verily I say unto you, This generation shall not pass, till all these things be fulfilled. Heaven and earth shall pass away, but my words shall not pass away." Matthew 24:34, 35.

NOTE—What Christ foretold of the destruction of Jerusalem came true to the very letter. Likewise may we be assured that what He has said about the end of the world will as certainly and as literally be fulfilled.

Who alone knows the exact day of Christ's coming?

"But of that day and hour *knoweth no man,* no, not the angels of heaven, but *my Father only."* Verse 36.

What moral conditions would precede Christ's second advent?

"But as the days of Noe were, so shall also the coming of the Son of man be. For as in the days that were before the flood they were *eating* and *drinking, marrying* and *giving in marriage,* until the day that Noe entered into the ark, and knew not until the flood came, and took them all away; *so shall also the coming of the Son of man be."* Verses 37-39.

What important admonition has Christ given us?

"Therefore *be ye also ready:* for in such an hour as ye think not the Son of man cometh." Verse 44.

What will be the experience of those who say in their hearts that the Lord is not soon coming?

"If that evil servant shall say in his heart, My lord delayeth his coming; and shall begin to smite his fellowservants, and to eat and drink with the drunken; the lord of that servant shall come in a day when he looketh not for him, and in an hour that he is not aware of, and shall cut him asunder ["cut him off," margin], and appoint him his portion with the hypocrites: there shall be weeping and gnashing of teeth." Verses 48-51.

Good News About
THE COMING KING

What promise did Christ make concerning His coming?

"Let not your heart be troubled: ye believe in God, believe also in me. In my Father's house are many mansions: if it were not so, I would have told you. I go to prepare a place for you. And if I go and prepare a place for you, *I will come again,* and receive you unto myself; that where I am, there ye may be also." John 14:1-3.

What follows the signs of Christ's coming?

"And then shall they see *the Son of man coming in a cloud with power and great glory."* Luke 21:27.

ANGELS AND APOSTLES PROCLAIM IT

At His ascension, how was Christ's return promised?

"And while they looked stedfastly toward heaven as he went up, behold, two men stood by them in white apparel; which also said, Ye men of Galilee, why stand ye gazing up into heaven? *this same Jesus, which is taken up from you into heaven, shall so come in like manner as ye have seen him go into heaven."* Acts 1:10, 11.

How does Paul give expression to this hope?

"Looking for that blessed hope, and the glorious appearing of the great God and our Saviour Jesus Christ." Titus 2:13.

What is Peter's testimony regarding it?

"We have not followed cunningly devised fables, when we made known unto you the power and coming of our Lord Jesus Christ, but were eyewitnesses of his majesty." 2 Peter 1:16.

THE UNPREPARED

Will the inhabitants of the earth as a whole be prepared to meet Him?

"Then shall appear the sign of the Son of man in heaven: and *then shall all the tribes of the earth mourn,* and they shall see the Son of man coming in the clouds of heaven with power and great glory." Matthew 24:30. "Behold, he cometh with clouds; and every eye shall see him, and they also which pierced him: and *all kindreds of the earth shall wail because of him."* Revelation 1:7.

Why will many not be prepared for this event?

"But and if that evil servant shall say in his heart, *My lord delayeth his coming;* and shall begin to smite his fellowservants, and to eat and drink with the drunken; the lord of that servant shall come in a day when he looketh not for him, and in an hour that he is not aware of, and shall cut him asunder, and appoint him his portion with the hypocrites: there shall be weeping and gnashing of teeth." Matthew 24:48-51.

What will the world be doing when Christ comes?

"But as the days of Noe were, so shall also the coming of the Son of man be. For as in the days that were before the flood *they were eating and drinking, marrying and giving in marriage,* until the day that Noe entered into the ark, and knew not until the flood came, and took them all away; so shall also the coming of the Son of man be." Verses 37-39. "Likewise also as it was in the days of Lot; *they did eat, they drank, they bought, they sold, they planted, they builded;* but the same day that Lot went out of Sodom it rained fire and brimstone from heaven, and destroyed them all. Even thus shall it be in the day when the Son of man is revealed." Luke 17:28-30.

NOTE—These texts do not teach that it is wrong in itself to eat, drink, marry, buy, sell, plant, or build, but that men's minds will be so taken up with these things that they will give little or no thought to the future life, and make no plans or preparation to meet Jesus when he comes.

Who is it that blinds men to the gospel of Christ?

"In whom *the god of this world* [Satan] hath blinded the minds of them which believe not, lest the light of the glorious gospel of Christ, who is the image of God, should shine unto them." 2 Corinthians 4:4.

NOTE—"To my mind this precious doctrine—for such I must call it—of the return of the Lord to this earth is taught in the New Testament as clearly as any other doctrine in it; yet I was in the Church fifteen or sixteen years before I ever heard a sermon on it. There is hardly any church that doesn't make a great deal of baptism, but in all of Paul's epistles I believe baptism is only spoken of thirteen times, while it speaks about the return of our Lord fifty times; and yet the Church has had very little to say about it. Now, I can see a reason for this; the devil does not want us to see this truth, for nothing would wake up the Church so much. The moment a man takes hold of the truth that Jesus Christ is coming back again to receive his followers to himself, this world loses its hold upon him. Gas stocks and water stocks and stocks in banks and railroads are of very much less consequence to him then. his heart is free, and he looks for the blessed appearing of his Lord, who, at his coming, will take him into his blessed Kingdom."—D. L. MOODY, *The Second Coming of Christ* (Revell), pp. 6, 7.

"'This same Jesus, which is taken up from you into heaven, *shall so come in like manner as ye have seen him go into heaven,'* is the parting promise of Jesus to his disciples, communicated through the two men in white apparel, as a cloud received him out of their sight. When after more than fifty years in glory he breaks the silence and speaks once more in the Revelation which he gave to his servant John, the post-ascension Gospel which he sends opens with, *'Behold, he cometh with clouds,'* and closes with *'Surely I come quickly.'* Considering the solemn emphasis thus laid upon this doctrine, and considering the great prominence given to it throughout the teaching of our Lord and of his apostles, how was it that for the first five years of my pastoral life it had absolutely no place in my preaching? Undoubtedly the reason lay in the lack of early instruction. Of all the sermons heard from childhood on, I do not remember listening to a single one upon this subject."—A. J. GORDON, *How Christ Came to Church,* pp. 44, 45.

PREPARED FOR HIS COMING

When are the saved to be like Jesus?

"Beloved, now are we the sons of God, and it doth not yet appear what we shall be: but we know that, *when he shall appear, we shall be like him;* for we shall see him as he is." 1 John 3:2.

Will Christ's coming be a time of reward?

"For the Son of man shall come in the glory of his Father with his angels; and *then he shall reward every man according to his works."* Matthew 16:27. "And, behold, I come quickly; *and my reward is with me,* to give every man according as his work shall be." Revelation 22:12.

To whom is salvation promised at Christ's appearing?

"So Christ was once offered to bear the sins of many; and *unto them that look for him* shall he appear the second time without sin unto salvation." Hebrews 9:28.

What influence has this hope upon the life?

"We know that, when he shall appear, we shall be like him; for we shall see him as he is. And *every man that hath this hope in him purifieth himself, even as he is pure."* 1 John 3:2, 3.

To whom is a crown of righteousness promised?

"For I am now ready to be offered, and the time of my departure is at hand. I have fought a good fight, I have finished my course, I have kept the faith: henceforth there is laid up for me a crown of righteousness, which the Lord, the righteous judge, shall give me at that day: and not to me only, but *unto all them also that love his appearing."* 2 Timothy 4:6-8.

What will the waiting ones say when Jesus comes?

"And it shall be said in that day, Lo, this is our God; we have waited for him, and he will save us: this is the Lord; we have waited for him, we will be glad and rejoice in his salvation." Isaiah 25:9.

Has the exact time of Christ's coming been revealed?

"But of that day and hour *knoweth no man,* no, not the angels of heaven, but my Father only." Matthew 24:36.

In view of this fact, what does Christ tell us to do?

"Watch therefore: for ye know not what hour your Lord doth come." Verse 42.

NOTE—"To the secure and careless he will come as a thief in the night: to his own, as their Lord."—HENRY ALFORD, *The New Testament for English Readers,* vol. 1, part 1, p. 170. "The proper attitude of a Christian is to be always looking for his Lord's return."—D. L. MOODY, *The Second Coming of Christ* (Revell), p. 9.

What warning has Christ given that we might not be taken by surprise by this great event?

"And take heed to yourselves, lest at any time your hearts be overcharged with surfeiting, and drunkenness, and cares of this life, and so that day come upon you unawares. For as a snare shall it come on all them that dwell on the face of the whole earth. Watch ye therefore, and pray always, that ye may be accounted worthy to escape all these things that shall come to pass, and to stand before the Son of man." Luke 21:34-36.

What Christian grace are we exhorted to exercise in our expectant longing for this event?

"Be *patient* therefore, brethren, unto the coming of the Lord. Behold, the husbandman waiteth for the precious fruit of the earth, and hath long patience for it, until he receive the early and latter rain. Be ye also *patient;* stablish your hearts: for the coming of the Lord draweth nigh." James 5:7, 8.

What has been the general attitude of Christians toward the second coming of Christ?

The belief of the Christian church in the second coming of Christ appears in Christian literature from the origin of the so-called Apostles' Creed down through to very recent times.

NOTE—These creeds can be found in the classic work *The Creeds of Christendom* (Harper) by the great church historian Philip Schaff. From that work we quote but two examples:

"The Nicene Creed is the first which obtained universal authority. It rests on older forms used in different churches of the East, and has undergone again some changes. . . . The original

Nicene Creed dates from the first ecumenical Council, which was held at Nicaea, A.D. 325."—vol. 1, pp. 24, 25. The text from which we quote is the original text of A.D. 325:

"We believe in . . . one Lord Jesus Christ, . . . who . . . suffered, and the third day he rose again, ascended into heaven; from thence *He shall come* to judge the quick and the dead."—*Ibid.,* pp. 28, 29.

The New Hampshire Baptist Confession (1833), which is "widely accepted by Baptists, especially in the Northern and Western States" *(ibid.,* vol. 3, p. 742), says:

"We believe that the end of the world is approaching; that *at the last day Christ will descend from heaven, and raise the dead from the grave to final retribution;* that a solemn separation will then take place; that the wicked will be adjudged to endless punishment, and the righteous to endless joy; and that this judgment will fix forever the final state of men in heaven or hell, on principles of righteousness."—*Ibid.,* p. 748.

DOES CHRIST COME AT TIME OF DEATH?

Did the early disciples think that death would be the second coming of Christ?

"Peter seeing him [John] saith to Jesus, Lord, and what shall this man do? Jesus saith unto him, If I will that he tarry *till I come,* what is that to thee? follow thou me. Then went this saying abroad among the brethren, that that disciple *should not die:* yet Jesus said not unto him, He shall not die; but, If I will that he tarry till I come, what is that to thee?" John 21:21-23.

NOTE—From this it is evident that the early disciples regarded death and the coming of Christ as two separate events. "'Therefore be ye also ready: for in such an hour as ye think not the Son of man cometh.' Some people say that means death; but the Word of God does not say it means death. Death is our enemy, but our Lord hath the keys of Death; he has conquered death, hell and the grave. . . . Christ is the Prince of Life; there is no death where he is; death flees at his coming; dead bodies sprang to life when he touched them or spoke to them. his coming is not death; he is the resurrection and the life; when he sets up his kingdom there is to be no death, but life forevermore."—D. L. MOODY, *The Second Coming of Christ* (Revell), pp. 10, 11.

CHRIST AND ANGELS TESTIFY

At His ascension, how did the angels say Christ would come again?

"When he had spoken these things, while they beheld, he was taken up; and *a cloud received him out of their sight.* And while they looked stedfastly toward heaven as he went up, behold, two men stood

by them in white apparel; which also said, Ye men of Galilee, why stand ye gazing up into heaven? this same Jesus, which is taken up from you into heaven, *shall so come in like manner as ye have seen him go into heaven."* Acts 1:9-11.

How did Christ Himself say He would come?

"For the Son of man shall come *in the glory of his Father with his angels."* Matthew 16:27. "Then shall all the tribes of the earth mourn, and they shall see the Son of man coming *in the clouds of heaven with power and great glory."* Matthew 24:30.

APOSTLES JOHN AND PAUL SPEAK

How many will see Him when He comes?

"Behold, he cometh with clouds; and *every eye shall see him,* and they also which pierced him." Revelation 1:7.

NOTE—Christ's second coming will be as real as was His first, and as visible as His ascension, and far more glorious. To spiritualize our Lord's return is to pervert the obvious meaning of His promise, "I will come again," and nullify the whole plan of redemption; for the reward of the faithful of all ages is to be given at this most glorious of all events.

What demonstration will accompany His coming?

"The Lord himself shall descend from heaven *with a shout, with the voice of the archangel, and with the trump of God:* and the dead in Christ shall rise first." 1 Thessalonians 4:16.

JESUS WARNS OF DECEPTION

What warning has Christ given concerning false views?

"Then if any man shall say unto you, *Lo, here is Christ, or there; believe it not.* For there shall arise false Christs, and false prophets, and shall shew great signs and wonders; insomuch that, if it were possible, they shall deceive the very elect. Behold, I have told you before. Wherefore if they shall say unto you, Behold, he is in the *desert;* go not forth: behold, he is in the *secret chambers;* believe it not." Matthew 24:23-26.

How visible is His coming to be?

"For as the lightning cometh out of the east, and shineth even unto the west; so shall also the coming of the Son of man be." Verse 27.

Good News About
THE CREATOR

HOW THE SABBATH WAS MADE

When and by whom was the Sabbath made?

"Thus the heavens and the earth were finished, and all the host of them. And *on the seventh day God ended his work* which he had made; *and he rested on the seventh day* from all his work which he had made." Genesis 2:1, 2.

What is the reason for keeping the Sabbath day holy?

"For in six days the Lord made heaven and earth, the sea, and all that in them is, and rested the seventh day: wherefore the Lord blessed the Sabbath day, and hallowed it." Exodus 20:11.

NOTE—The Sabbath is the memorial of Creation, the sign of God's creative power. God designed that through keeping it man should forever remember him as the true and living God, the Creator of all things.

On the perpetuity of the Sabbath command, Wesley declared, "'Six days shalt thou do all manner of work. But the seventh day is the Sabbath of the Lord thy God.' It is not thine, but God's day. he claims it for his own. he always did claim it for his own, even from the beginning of the world. 'In six days the Lord made heaven and earth, and rested the seventh day. Therefore the Lord blessed the Sabbath-day and hallowed it.' He *hallowed* it; that is, he made it holy; he reserved it for his own service. He appointed, that as long as the sun or the moon, the heavens and the earth, should endure, the children of men should spend this day in the worship of him who 'gave them life and breath and all things.'"—JOHN WESLEY, "A Word to a Sabbath-Breaker," in *Works,* vol. 11 (1830 ed.), pp. 164-166.

Did Christ have anything to do with Creation and the making of the Sabbath?

"All things were made *by him;* and *without him was not any thing made that was made."* John 1:3. (See also Ephesians 3:9; Colossians 1:16; Hebrews 1:2.)

NOTE—Christ was the active agent in creation. The Creator rested on the seventh day from the work of creation; therefore, Christ must have rested on the seventh day with the Father. Consequently, it is His rest day as well as the Father's.

After resting on the seventh day, what did God do?

"And God *blessed the seventh day, and sanctified it:* because that in it he had rested from all his work which God created and made." Genesis 2:3.

NOTE—By three distinct acts, then, was the Sabbath made: God *rested* on it; He *blessed* it; He *sanctified* it. *Sanctify* means "to make sacred or holy," "to consecrate," "to set apart as sacred."

MAN AND THE SABBATH

For whom did Christ say the Sabbath was made?

"And he said unto them, *The sabbath was made for man,* and not man for the sabbath." Mark 2:27.

NOTE—*Man* here means "mankind." God instituted the Sabbath to be a source of benefit and blessing to the human family.

"Jesus says: 'The Sabbath was made for man;' and the necessary inference is that from the beginning man knew the primary uses of the day, and received the benefits which it was designed to impart. . . .

"Before the giving of the law from Sinai the obligation of the Sabbath was understood."—J. J. TAYLOR (Baptist), *The Sabbatic Question* (Revell, 1914 ed.), pp. 20-24.

"I honestly believe that this commandment is just as binding to-day as it ever was. I have talked with men who have said that it has been abrogated, but they have never been able to point to any place in the Bible where God repealed it. When Christ was on earth, He did nothing to set it aside; He freed it from the traces under which the scribes and Pharisees had put it, and gave it its true place. 'The sabbath was made for man, not man for the sabbath.' It is just as practicable and as necessary for men to-day as it ever was—in fact, more than ever, because we live in such an intense age.

"The sabbath was binding in Eden, and it has been in force ever since. This fourth commandment begins with the word 'remember,' showing that the sabbath already existed when God wrote this law on the tables of stone at Sinai. How can men claim that this one commandment has been done away with when they will admit that the other nine are still binding?"—D. L. MOODY, *Weighed and Wanting* (1898 ed.), pp. 46, 47.

When did God bless and sanctify the seventh day?

"And on the seventh day God ended his work which he had made; and he rested on the seventh day from all his work which he had made. And God blessed the seventh day, and sanctified it: *because that in it he* had *rested from all his work* which God created and made." Genesis 2:2, 3.

NOTE—"If we had no other passage than this of Genesis 2:3, there would be no difficulty in deducing from it a precept for the universal observance of a Sabbath, or seventh day, to be devoted to God as holy time, by all of that race for whom the earth and its nature were specially prepared.

The First Sabbath
Harry Anderson, Artist

The first men must have known it. The words 'He hallowed it' can have no meaning otherwise. They would be a blank unless in reference to some who were required to keep it holy."—JOHN PETER LANGE, *A Commentary on the Holy Scriptures,* on Genesis 2:3, vol. 1, p. 197.

THE SABBATH TEST IN ISRAEL

What does the Sabbath commandment require?

"Remember the sabbath day, to keep it holy. Six days shalt thou labour, and do all thy work: but the seventh day is the sabbath of the Lord thy God: *in it thou shalt not do any work,* thou, nor thy son, nor thy daughter, thy manservant, nor thy maidservant, nor thy cattle, nor thy stranger that is within thy gates." Exodus 20:8-10.

NOTE—Luther says, on Exodus 16:4, 22-30: "Hence you can see that the Sabbath was before the law of Moses came, and has existed from the beginning of the world. Especially have the devout, who have preserved the true faith, met together and called upon God on this day."—Translated from *Auslegung des Alten Testaments* (Commentary on the Old Testament), in *Sämmtliche Schriften* (Collected Writings), edited by J. G. Walch, vol. 3, col. 950.

How did God prove Israel in the wilderness?

"I will rain bread from heaven for you; and the people shall go out and gather a certain rate every day, *that I may prove them, whether they will walk in my law, or no."* Exodus 16:4.

On which day was a double portion of manna gathered?

"And it came to pass, that *on the sixth day they gathered twice as much bread,* two omers for one man." Verse 22.

What did Moses say to the rulers?

"This is that which the Lord hath said, To morrow is the rest of the holy sabbath unto the Lord." Verse 23.

NOTE—"2. The Sabbath is indispensable to man, being promotive of his highest good, physically, intellectually, socially, spiritually, and eternally. Hence its observance is connected with the best of promises, and its violation with the severest penalties. Ex. 23:12; 31:12-18; Neh. 13:15-22; Isa. 56:2-7; 58:13-14; Jer. 17:21-27; Eze. 20:12, 13; 22:26-31. Its sanctity was very distinctly marked in the gathering of the manna. Ex. 16:22-30.

"3. The original law of the Sabbath was renewed and made a prominent part of the moral law, or ten commandments, given through Moses at Sinai. Ex. 20:8-11."—AMOS BINNEY AND DANIEL STEELE, *Binney's Theological Compend Improved* (1902 ed.), p. 170.

What did some of the people do on the seventh day?

"It came to pass, that *there went out some of the people on the seventh day for to gather,* and they found none." Verse 27.

How did God reprove their disobedience?

"And the Lord said unto Moses, *How long refuse ye to keep my commandments and my laws?"* Verse 28.

Why was twice as much manna given on the sixth day?

"See, *for that the Lord hath given you the sabbath, therefore he giveth you on the sixth day the bread of two days;* abide ye every man in his place, let no man go out of his place on the seventh day." Verse 29.

How, then, did the Lord test the people?

Over the keeping of the Sabbath.

NOTE—Thus we see that the Sabbath commandment was a part of God's law before this law was spoken from Sinai, for this incident occurred before Israel came to Sinai. Both the Sabbath and the law existed from Creation.

"As presented to us in the Scriptures the Sabbath was not the invention of any religious founder. It was not at first part of any system of religion, but an entirely independent institution. Very definitely it is presented in Genesis as the very first institution, inaugurated by the Creator himself. It was purely religious, wholly moral, wholly spiritual. It had no prescribed ceremonies, no sacramentarian significance. It required no priest, no liturgy. It was for man as God's creature, steward and friend."—W. O. CARVER, *Sabbath Observance,* p. 41. Copyright, 1940, by the Sunday School Board of the Southern Baptist Convention. Used by permission.

GOD'S MEMORIAL

What is to endure throughout all generations?

"Thy name, O Lord, endureth for ever; and thy memorial, O Lord, throughout all generations." Psalm 135:13. Memorial: "Anything . . . intended to preserve the memory of a person or event."—*Webster's Collegiate Dictionary* (5th ed., 1935), p. 624.

What illustration of a memorial is given in the Bible?

"And this day shall be unto you for a memorial; and ye shall keep it a feast to the Lord throughout your generations; ye shall keep it a feast by an ordinance for ever." Exodus 12:14.

NOTE—This, the Passover, was a periodical memorial, to be observed on the fourteenth day of the first month of each year, the day on which the Israelites were delivered from Egyptian bondage, and its celebration was to be, with the seven days' feast of unleavened bread following and connected with it, in commemoration of that event. (See Exodus 13:3-9.)

GOD'S MEMORIAL OF CREATION

Does God design the Creation to be remembered?

"The works of the Lord are great, sought out of all them that have pleasure therein. His work is honourable and glorious: and his righteousness endureth for ever. He hath made his wonderful works to be re-membered." Psalm 111:2-4.

What has He commanded men to observe in memory of this great work?
"Remember the sabbath day, to keep it holy. . . . For in six days the Lord made heaven and earth, the sea, and all that in them is, and rested the seventh day: wherefore the Lord blessed the sabbath day, and hallowed it." Exodus 20:8-11.

Of what was this memorial to be a sign?
"And hallow my sabbaths; and they shall be a sign between me and you, that ye may know that I am the Lord your God." Ezekiel 20:20.

How long was the Sabbath to be a sign of the true God?
"It is a sign between me and the children of Israel for ever: for in six days the Lord made heaven and earth, and on the seventh day he rested, and was refreshed." Exodus 31:17.

NOTE—It is manifest that if the object of the Sabbath was to remember God as the Creator, and it had been faith-fully kept from the first, there would not now be a heathen or an idolater on the face of the earth.

What besides Creation were the Israelites to remember when they kept the Sabbath?
"And remember that thou wast a servant in the land of Egypt, and that the Lord thy God brought thee out thence through a mighty hand and by a stretched out arm: therefore the Lord thy God commanded thee to keep the sabbath day." Deuteronomy 5:15.

NOTE—There is a deep significance to this scripture. In Egypt, through oppression and idolatrous surroundings, the keeping of the Sabbath had become not only almost obso-lete but well-nigh impossible. They were delivered from bondage in order that they might keep God's law (Psalm 105:43-45), and particularly the Sabbath, the great seal, sign, and memorial institution of the law. The recollection of their bondage and oppressed condition in Egypt was to be an additional incentive for keeping the Sabbath in the land of freedom. The Sabbath, therefore, besides being a memorial of Creation, was to be to them a memorial of their deliverance from bondage, and of the great power of God as manifested in this deliverance. And as Egypt stands as a symbol of the condition of everyone in the world under the slavery of sin, so the Sabbath is to be kept by every saved soul as a memorial of the deliverance from this slavery by the mighty power of God through Christ.

Of what else does God say He gave the Sabbath to His people to be a sign, or reminder?
"Moreover also I gave them my sabbaths, to be a sign between me and them, that they might know that I am the Lord that sanctify them." Ezekiel 20:12.

NOTE—Sanctification is a work of redemption—of making holy sinful or unholy beings. Like the work of Creation itself, this requires creative power. (See Psalm 51:10; John 3:3, 6; Ephesians 2:10.) And as the Sabbath is the appropriate sign, or memorial, of the creative power of God wherever displayed, whether in Creation, deliverance from human bondage, or deliverance from the slavery of sin, it is to be kept as a sign of the work of sanctification. This will be one great reason for the saints keeping it throughout eternity. It will remind them not only of their own creation and the creation of the universe but also of their redemption.

Through whom do we have sanctification?
"But of him are ye in Christ Jesus, who of God is made unto us wisdom, and righteousness, and sanc-tification, and redemption." 1 Corinthians 1:30.

NOTE—Then, as the Sabbath is a sign, or memorial, of sanctification, and as Christ is the one through whom the work of sanctification is accomplished, the Sabbath is a sign, or memorial, of what Christ is to the believer. Through the Sabbath, therefore, God designed that the believer and Christ should be very closely linked together.

In heaven, how often will the redeemed congre-gate to worship the Lord?
"For as the new heavens and the new earth, which I will make, shall remain before me, saith the Lord, so shall your seed and your name remain. And it shall come to pass, that from one new moon to another, and from one sabbath to another, shall all flesh come to worship before me, saith the Lord." Isaiah 66:22, 23.

NOTE—The Sabbath, which is the memorial of God's creative power, will never cease to exist. When this sinful state of things shall give way to the sinless new earth, the fact upon which the Sabbath institution is based will still re-main; and those who shall be permitted to live in the new earth will still commemorate the creative power of God, while singing the song of Moses and the Lamb. (Revelation 15:3. See Revelation 22:1, 2.)

MAKER AND KEEPER OF THE SABBATH

Of what did Christ say the Son of man is Lord?
"The Son of man is Lord even *of the sabbath day.*" Matthew 12:8. (See also Mark 2:28.)

Who made the Sabbath?
"All things were made *by him* [Christ, the Word]." John 1:3.

NOTE—Christ was the creative agent.

Did Christ, while on earth, keep the Sabbath?
"As his custom was, *he went into the synagogue on the sabbath day, and stood up for to read.*" Luke 4:16.

Although Lord, Maker, and an observer of the Sabbath, how was He watched and spied upon on this day?
"And the scribes and Pharisees watched him, *whether he would heal on the sabbath day;* that they

might find an accusation against him." Luke 6:7.

How did Christ meet their false ideas of Sabbath-keeping?

"Then said Jesus, . . . *Is it lawful on the sabbath days to do good, or to do evil? to save life, or to destroy it?"* Verse 9.

How did they manifest their displeasure at His healing the man with the withered hand on the Sabbath?

"And they were *filled with madness;* and *communed one with another what they might do to Jesus."* Verse 11. "And the Pharisees went forth, and straightway *took counsel . . . , how they might destroy him."* Mark 3:6.

> NOTE—Although the miracle Christ performed had given evidence that He was from God, they were angry because He had shown *their views of Sabbathkeeping to be wrong.* Wounded pride, obstinacy, and malice, therefore, combined to fill them with *madness;* and they went out immediately and held counsel with the Herodians—their political enemies—for the purpose of accomplishing His death.

Because Jesus healed a man on the Sabbath day, and told him to take up his bed and walk, what did the Jews do?

"Therefore did the Jews *persecute* Jesus, and *sought to slay him,* because he had done these things on the sabbath day." John 5:16.

> NOTE—It is noteworthy that not the least of the malice which finally caused his crucifixion was engendered over this very question of Sabbath observance. Christ did not keep the Sabbath according to their ideas, and so they sought to kill him. Many today cherish this same spirit. Because some do not agree with their ideas of the Sabbath, or Sabbath observance, they seek to persecute and oppress them—seek laws, and alliances with political powers, to compel respect for their views.

How did Jesus answer them?

"But Jesus answered them, *My Father worketh hitherto, and I work."* Verse 17.

> NOTE—The ordinary operations of nature, as manifested in God's almighty, upholding, beneficent, and healing power, continue on the Sabbath. To cooperate with God and nature in the work of healing on the Sabbath cannot, therefore, be out of harmony with God's Sabbath law.

What effect did this answer have upon the Jews?

"Therefore the Jews *sought the more to kill him."* Verse 18.

Because the disciples plucked a few heads of grain on the Sabbath day to satisfy hunger, what did the Pharisees say?

"And the Pharisees said unto him, *Behold, why do they on the sabbath day that which is not lawful?"* Mark 2:24.

What was Christ's reply?

"And he said unto them, have ye never read what David did, when he had need, and was an hungred, he, and they that were with him? how he . . . did eat the shewbread, which is not lawful to eat but for the priests, and gave also to them which were with him? And he said unto them, *The sabbath was made for man, and not man for the sabbath."* Verses 25-27.

What was said of Christ's healing a woman one Sabbath?

"The ruler of the synagogue answered, . . . *There are six days in which men ought to work: in them therefore come and be healed, and not on the sabbath day."* Luke 13:14.

What was Christ's answer?

"Thou hypocrite, doth not each one of you on the sabbath loose his ox or his ass from the stall, and lead him away to watering? and ought not this woman, being a daughter of Abraham, whom Satan hath bound, lo, these eighteen years, be loosed from this bond on the sabbath day?" Verses 15, 16.

What effect did Christ's answers have upon the people?

"All his adversaries were ashamed: and all the people rejoiced for all the glorious things that were done by him." Verse 17.

How did Christ justify acts of mercy on the Sabbath?

"What man shall there be among you, that shall have one sheep, and if it fall into a pit on the sabbath day, will he not lay hold on it, and lift it out? How much then is a man better than a sheep? Wherefore it is lawful to do well on the sabbath days." Matthew 12:11, 12. (See also Luke 14:5, 6.)

> NOTE—"Jesus observed the Sabbath Day of his own people. It was his custom to worship in the synagogues on the Sabbath Day. After he entered upon his own ministry, he and his followers continued to recognize and use the Sabbath Day, but according to his own individual and spiritual insight and interpretation. Even when Sabbath observance was made one of the chief grounds of bitter antagonism to him by the Pharisees he continued his recognition of the Sabbath and uttered no word that can properly be construed as lacking in deep reverence. Apparently, he expected that his followers would continue to hold and inculcate the spirit of the historic Sabbath."—W. O. CARVER, *Sabbath Observance,* p. 25. Copyright, 1940, by the Sunday School Board of the Southern Baptist Convention. Used by permission.

What dispute did Christ's miracles cause?

"Therefore said some of the Pharisees, *This man is not of God, because he keepeth not the sabbath day. Others said, How can a man that is a sinner do such miracles?"* John 9:16.

NOTE—By these miracles God was setting the seal of His approval to Christ's views and teachings respecting the Sabbath, and to His manner of observing it, and thus condemning the narrow and false views of the Pharisees. Hence the division.

JESUS MAGNIFIES THE SABBATH

According to Isaiah, what was Christ to do with the law?

"He will *magnify* the law, and *make it honourable.*" Isaiah 42:21.

NOTE—In nothing, perhaps, was this more strikingly fulfilled than in the matter of Sabbath observance. By their numerous traditional regulations and senseless restrictions the Jews had made the Sabbath a burden, and anything but a delight. Christ removed all these, and by His life and teachings restored the Sabbath to its proper place as a day of worship, of contemplation of God, a day for doing acts of charity and mercy. Thus He magnified it and made it honorable. One of the most prominent features of Christ's ministry was this work of *Sabbath reform.* Christ did not *abolish* or *change* the Sabbath; but He did rescue it from the rubbish of tradition, false ideas, and superstitions by which it had been degraded. The Pharisees had placed the institution *above* man and *against* man. Christ reversed the order, and said, "The sabbath was made *for man* and not man *for the sabbath."* He showed that it was to minister to the happiness and well-being of both man and beast.

In view of the coming destruction and desolation of the city of Jerusalem, for what did Christ tell His disciples to pray?

"But pray ye that your flight be not in the winter, *neither on the sabbath day."* Matthew 24:20.

NOTE—"Christ is here speaking of the flight of the apostles and other Christians out of Jerusalem and Judea, just before their final destruction, as is manifest by the whole context, and especially by the 16th verse: 'Then let them which be in Judea flee into the mountains.' But the final destruction of Jerusalem was after the dissolution of the Jewish constitution, and after the Christian dispensation was fully set up. Yet it is plainly implied in these words of the Lord, that even then Christians were bound to a strict observation of the Sabbath."—JONATHAN EDWARDS, *Works* (reprint of Worcester ed., 1844-1848), vol. 4, pp. 621, 622.

"The Great Teacher never intimated that the Sabbath was a ceremonial ordinance to cease with the Mosaic ritual. . . . Instead of anticipating its extinction along with the ceremonial law, he speaks of its existence after the downfall of Jerusalem. [See Matthew 24:20.]"—W. D. KILLEN (Irish Presbyterian), *The Ancient Church* (1883 ed.), p. 188.

SABBATH AND THE CROSS

What day immediately precedes the first day of the week?

"In the end of *the sabbath,* as it began to dawn toward the first day of the week." Matthew 28:1.

NOTE—According to the New Testament, therefore, the Sabbath had passed when the first day of the week began.

After the Crucifixion, what day was kept by the women who followed Jesus?

"They returned, and prepared spices and ointments; and *rested the sabbath day according to the commandment."* Luke 23:56.

When is the Sabbath, "according to the commandment"?

"But *the seventh day is the sabbath* of the Lord thy God." Exodus 20:10.

JESUS AND THE SABBATH

What was Christ's custom respecting the Sabbath?

"And he came to Nazareth, where he had been brought up: and, as his custom was, *he went into the synagogue on the sabbath day,* and stood up for to read." Luke 4:16.

In what instruction to His disciples did Christ recognize the existence of the Sabbath long after His ascension?

"But pray ye that your flight be not in the winter, *neither on the sabbath day."* Matthew 24:20.

NOTE—The flight of the Christians took place late in October, A.D. 66, three and one-half years before the fall of Jerusalem. For Jesus' attitude toward the Sabbath, see the preceding reading.

PAUL AND THE SABBATH

On what day did Paul and Barnabas preach at Antioch?

"They came to Antioch in Pisidia, and went into the synagogue on *the sabbath day."* Acts 13:14.

When did the Gentiles ask Paul to repeat his sermon?

"And when the Jews were gone out of the synagogue, the Gentiles besought that these words might be preached to them *the next sabbath."* Verse 42.

On what day did Paul preach to the women at Philippi?

"And *on the sabbath* we went out of the city by a river side, where prayer was wont to be made; and we sat down, and spake unto the women which resorted thither." Acts 16:13.

On what day did Paul preach to the Jews at Thessalonica?

"They came to Thessalonica, where was a synagogue of the Jews: and Paul, *as his manner was, went in unto them, and three sabbath days reasoned with them out of the scriptures."* Acts 17:1, 2.

NOTE—It was Paul's manner, as it was Christ's custom (Luke 4:16), to attend religious services on the Sabbath.

How did the apostle spend the working days of the week when at Corinth, and what did he do on the Sabbath?

"Because he was of the same craft, he abode with them, and *wrought:* for by their occupation they were *tentmakers."* Acts 18:3. (See Ezekiel 46:1.) "And *he reasoned in the synagogue every sabbath,* and persuaded the Jews and the Greeks." Acts 18:4.

NOTE—"He continued there *a year and six months,* teaching the word of God among them." Verse 11. These texts do not definitely prove that the apostle held seventy-eight Sabbath meetings in Corinth, but they show conclusively that it was his custom to observe that day by devoting it to religious purposes. The careful student will note that his reasoning in the synagogue every Sabbath applies only to the comparatively brief time during which he was permitted the use of the synagogue. But the history of the apostle's work in the book of Acts fully warrants us in believing that wherever he was, Paul utilized to the full every opportunity to pursue his gospel work on the Sabbath. The same is true, not only of the apostles, but of most Christians during the first three centuries.

JOHN AND THE LORD'S DAY

On what day was John in the Spirit?

"I was in the Spirit *on the Lord's day."* Revelation 1:10.

Who is Lord of the Sabbath?

"The Son of man is Lord also of the sabbath." Mark 2:28.

What, through Isaiah, does the Lord call the Sabbath?

"If thou turn away thy foot from the sabbath, from doing thy pleasure on *my holy day."* Isaiah 58:13.

Why does the Lord call the Sabbath His day?

"For in six days the Lord made heaven and earth, the sea, and all that in them is, and *rested the seventh day:* wherefore the Lord *blessed the sabbath day, and hallowed it."* Exodus 20:11.

Through whom did God create the world?

"God . . . hath in these last days spoken unto us *by his Son, . . . by whom also he made the worlds."* Hebrews 1:1, 2.

NOTE—The Bible recognizes but one weekly Sabbath—the day upon which God rested in the beginning; which was made known to Israel at Sinai (Nehemiah 9:13, 14); was observed by Christ and His apostles; and is to be kept by the redeemed in the new earth (Isaiah 66:22, 23).

The terms *Sabbath, Sabbaths,* and *Sabbath days* occur sixty times in the New Testament, and in every case but one refer to the seventh day. In Colossians 2:16, 17, reference is made to the annual sabbaths connected with the three annual feasts observed by Israel before the first coming of Christ.

"The sacred name of the seventh day is Sabbath. This fact is too clear to require argument. The truth is stated in concise terms: 'The seventh day is the Sabbath of the Lord thy God.' This utterance is repeated in Exodus 16:26; 23:12; 31:15; 35:2; Leviticus 23:3; and Deuteronomy 5:14. On this point the plain teaching of the word has been admitted in all ages. Except to certain special sabbaths appointed in Levitical law, and these invariably governed by the month rather than the week, the Bible in all its utterances never, no, not once, applies the name Sabbath to any other day."—J. J. TAYLOR, *The Sabbatic Question* (Revell), pp. 16, 17.

The first day of the week is mentioned but eight times in the New Testament, six of which are found in the four Gospels, and refer to the day on which Christ arose from the dead. (See Matthew 28:1; Mark 16:2, 9; Luke 24:1; John 20:1, 19.) The other two (Acts 20:7; 1 Corinthians 16:2) refer to the only religious meeting held on the first day of the week after the ascension, in apostolic times, recorded in the New Testament, and to a systematic accounting and laying by in store at home on that day for the poor saints in Judea and Jerusalem.

It is evident, therefore, that the Sabbath of the New Testament is the same as the Sabbath of the Old Testament, and that there is nothing in the New Testament setting aside the seventh-day Sabbath and putting the first day of the week in its place.

Good News About
GOD'S UNCHANGEABLE DAY

THE SABBATH AND THE LAW

Of what is the Sabbath commandment a part?
The law of God. (See Exodus 20:8-11.)

What did Christ say of the law?
"Think not that I am come to destroy the law, or the prophets: I am not come to destroy, but to fulfil." Matthew 5:17.

NOTE—"He [Christ] fulfilled the moral law by obeying, by bringing out its fullness of meaning, by showing its intense spirituality, and He established it on a surer basis than ever as the eternal law of righteousness. He fulfilled the ceremonial and typical law, not only by conforming to its requirements, but by realizing its spiritual significance. He filled up the shadowy outlines of the types, and, thus fulfilled, they pass away, and it is no longer necessary for us to observe the Passover or slay the daily lamb: we have the substance in Christ."—*The International Standard Bible Encyclopedia,* vol. 3, p. 1847.

How enduring did He say the law is?
"Till heaven and earth pass, one jot or one tittle shall in no wise pass from the law, till all be fulfilled." Verse 18.

What did He say of those who break the commandments and teach others to do so?
"Whosoever therefore shall break one of these least commandments, and shall teach men so, *he shall be called the least in the kingdom of heaven."* Verse 19.

NOTE—From this it is evident that all ten commandments are binding in the Christian dispensation, and that Christ had no thought of changing any of them. One of these commands was the observance of the seventh day as the Sabbath. But most Christians keep the first day of the week instead.

"It is a remarkable and regrettable fact that while most Christians regard the decalogue as a whole as being of personal and perpetual obligation, so many should make the fourth commandment an exception. It is the most complete and comprehensive of them all and, unlike the rest, is expressed both positively and negatively."—W. C. PROCTER, in *Moody Bible Institute Monthly,* December 1933, p. 160.

Many believe that Christ changed the Sabbath. But, from His own words, we see that He came for no such purpose. The responsibility for this change must therefore be looked for elsewhere.

Those who believe that Jesus changed the Sabbath base it only on a supposition: "Jesus, after his resurrection, changed the Sabbath from the seventh to the first day of the week; thus showing his authority as Lord even of the Sabbath. . . . *When Jesus gave instructions for this change we are not told,* but very likely during the time when he spake to his apostles of the things pertaining to his kingdom. Acts 1:3. This is probably one of the many unrecorded things which Jesus did. John 20:30; 21:25."—AMOS BINNEY AND DANIEL STEELE (Methodist), *Binney's Theological Compend Improved,* p. 171.

What kind of worship does the Saviour call that which is not according to God's commandments?
"But *in vain they do worship me,* teaching for doctrines the commandments of men." Matthew 15:9.

HISTORY OF THE SABBATH

For how long a time was the seventh-day Sabbath observed in the Christian church?
For many centuries. In fact, its observance has never wholly ceased in the Christian church.

NOTE—Mr. Morer, a learned clergyman of the Church of England, says: "The *Primitive Christians* had a great veneration for the *Sabbath,* and spent the *Day* in Devotion and Sermons. And 'tis not to be doubted but they derived this Practice from the *Apostles* themselves."—*A Discourse in Six Dialogues on the Name, Notion, and Observation of the Lord's Day,* p. 189.

"A history of the problem shows that in some places, it was really only after some centuries that the Sabbath rest really was entirely abolished, and by that time the practice of observing a bodily rest on the Sunday had taken its place."—VINCENT J. KELLY, *Forbidden Sunday and Feast-Day Occupations,* p. 15.

Lyman Coleman says: "Down even to the fifth century the observance of the Jewish Sabbath was continued in the Christian church, but with a rigor and a solemnity gradually diminishing until it was wholly discontinued."—*Ancient Christianity Exemplified,* chap. 26, sec. 2.

The church historian Socrates, who wrote in the fifth century, says: "Almost all the churches throughout the world celebrate the sacred mysteries on the Sabbath of every week, yet the Christians of Alexandria and at Rome, on account of some ancient tradition, have ceased to do this."—*Ecclesiastical History,* book 5, chap. 22, in *A Select Library of Nicene and Post-Nicene Fathers,* 2nd series, vol. 2, p. 32.

Sozomen, another historian of the same period, writes: "The people of Constantinople, and almost everywhere, assemble together on the Sabbath, as well as on the first day of the week, which custom is never observed at Rome or at

Alexandria."—*Ecclesiastical History,* book 7, chap. 19, in the same volume as the above quotation.

All this would have been inconceivable had there been a divine command given for the change of the Sabbath.

SUNDAY OBSERVANCE

How did Sunday observance originate?

As a voluntary celebration of the resurrection, a custom without pretense of divine authority.

NOTE—"Opposition to Judaism introduced the particular festival of Sunday very early, indeed, into the place of the Sabbath. . . . The festival of Sunday, like all other festivals, was always only a human ordinance, and it was far from the intentions of the apostles to establish a Divine command in this respect, far from them, and from the early apostolic Church, to transfer the laws of the Sabbath to Sunday. Perhaps, at the end of the second century a false application of this kind had begun to take place; for men appear by that time to have considered labouring on Sunday as a sin."—AUGUSTUS NEANDER, *The History of the Christian Religion and Church* (Rose's translation from the first German ed.), p. 186.

"'The observance of the Sunday was at first supplemental to that of the Sabbath, but in proportion as the gulf between the Church and the Synagogue widened, the Sabbath became less and less important and ended at length in being entirely neglected.'"—L. DUCHESNE, *Christian Worship: Its Origin and Evolution* (tr. from the 4th French ed. by M. L. McClure, London, 1910), p. 47.

Who first enjoined Sundaykeeping by law?

Constantine the Great.

NOTE—"(1) That the Sunday was in the beginning not looked on as a day of bodily repose; nor was an analogy drawn between the Jewish Sabbath and the Christian Sunday, except as days of worship. . . .

"(3) The keeping of the Sunday rest arose from the custom of the people and the constitution of the Church. . . .

"(5) Tertullian was probably the first to refer to a cessation of worldly affairs on the Sunday; the Council of Laodicea issued the first conciliar legislation for that day; Constantine I issued the first civil legislation; St. Martin of Braga was probably the first to use the term 'servile work' in its present theological sense."—VINCENT J. KELLY, *Forbidden Sunday and Feast-Day Occupations,* p. 203.

"The earliest recognition of the observance of Sunday as a legal duty is a constitution of Constantine in 321 A.D., enacting that all courts of justice, inhabitants of towns, and workshops were to be at rest on Sunday *(venerabili die solis),* with an exception in favor of those engaged in agricultural labor."—*Encyclopaedia Britannica,* 11th ed., art. "Sunday."

"On the venerable Day of the Sun let the magistrates and people residing in cities rest, and let all workshops be closed. In the country, however, persons engaged in agriculture may freely and lawfully continue their pursuits; because it often happens that another day is not so suitable for grain sowing or for vine planting; lest by neglecting the proper moment for such operations the bounty of heaven should be lost. (Given the 7th day of March, Crispus and Constantine being consuls each of them for the second time.)"—*Codex Justinianus,* lib. 3, tit. 12, 3; translated in *History of the*

Christian Church, by Philip Schaff, D.D., (Scribners, 1902 ed.), vol. 3, p. 380.

This edict, issued by Constantine, who first opened the way for the union of church and state in the Roman Empire, in a manner supplied the lack of a divine command for Sunday observance. It was one of the important steps in bringing about and establishing the change of the Sabbath.

What does Eusebius say on this subject?

"All things whatsoever that it was duty to do on the Sabbath, these we [the church] have transferred to the Lord's day."—Translated from EUSEBIUS, *Commentary on the Psalm,* in Migne, *Patrologia Graeca,* vol. 23, cols. 1171, 1172.

NOTE—The change of the Sabbath was the result of the combined efforts of church and state, and it took centuries to accomplish it. Eusebius of Caesarea (270-338) was a noted bishop of the church, biographer and flatterer of Constantine, and the reputed father of ecclesiastical history.

By what church council was the observance of the seventh day forbidden and Sunday observance enjoined?

The Council of Laodicea, in Asia Minor, fourth century.

NOTE—Canon 29 reads: "Christians shall not Judaize and be idle on Saturday *[sabbato,* the Sabbath], but shall work on that day; but the Lord's day they shall especially honour, and, as being Christians, shall, if possible, do no work on that day. If, however, they are found Judaizing, they shall be shut out *[anathema]* from Christ."—CHARLES JOSEPH HEFELE, *A History of the Councils of the Church,* vol. 2 (1896 English ed.), p. 316.

The Puritan William Prynne said (1655) that "the Council of Laodicea . . . first set[t]led the observation of the Lords-day, and prohibited . . . the keeping of the Jewish Sabbath under an Anathema."—A *Briefe Polemicall Dissertation Concerning . . . the Lords-day-Sabbath,* p. 44.

What was done at the Council of Laodicea was but one of the steps by which the change of the Sabbath was effected. It was looked back upon as the first church council to forbid Sabbath observance and enjoin Sunday rest as far as possible, but it was not so strict as later decrees. Different writers give conflicting dates for this Council of Laodicea. The exact date is unknown, but may be placed "generally somewhere between the years 343 and 381." (Hefele, vol. 2, p. 298.)

Have church leaders claimed to have changed the Sabbath?

Yes. The Catholic Church has claimed responsibility for this change.

NOTE—The *Catechismus Romanus* was commanded by the Council of Trent and published by the Vatican Press, by order of Pope Pius V, in 1566. This catechism for priests says: "It pleased the church of God, that the religious celebration of the Sabbath day should be transferred to 'the Lord's day.'"—*Catechism of the Council of Trent* (Donovan's translation 1867), part 3, chap. 4, p. 345. The same, in slightly different wording, is in the McHugh and Callan translation (1937 ed.), p. 402.

"The pope is of so great authority and power that he can

Constantine and the Sunday Law
Jim Padgett, Artist

modify, explain, or interpret even divine laws. . . . The pope can modify divine law, since his power is not of man, but of God, and he acts as vicegerent of God upon earth."—Translated from LUCIUS FERRARIS, *Prompta Bibliotheca* (Ready Library), "Papa," art. 2.

"*Ques.*—How prove you that the Church hath power to command feasts and holydays?

"*Ans.*—By the very act of changing the Sabbath into Sunday, which Protestants allow of; and therefore they fondly contradict themselves, by keeping Sunday strictly, and breaking most other feasts commanded by the same Church.—HENRY TUBERVILLE, *An Abridgment of the Christian Doctrine* (1833 approbation), p. 58. (Same statement in *Manual of Christian Doctrine,* Ed. by Daniel Ferris [1916 ed.], p. 67.)

"*Ques.*—Have you any other way of proving that the Church has power to institute festivals of precept?

"*Ans.*—Had she not such power, she could not have done that in which all modern religionists agree with her;—she could not have substituted the observance of Sunday, the first day of the week, for the observance of Saturday, the seventh day, a change for which there is no Scriptural authority.—STEPHEN KEENAN, *A Doctrinal Catechism* (3rd ed.), p. 174.

"The Catholic Church, . . . by virtue of her divine mission, changed the day from Saturday to Sunday."—*The Catholic Mirror,* official organ of Cardinal Gibbons, Sept. 23, 1893.

"1. Is Saturday the 7th day according to the Bible and the 10 Commandments?

"**I** answer yes.

"2. Is Sunday the first day of the week, and did the Church change the 7th day—Saturday—for Sunday, the 1st. day?

"**I** answer yes.

"3. Did Christ change the day?

"**I** answer no! Faithfully yours,

"J. Card. Gibbons"—Gibbons' Autograph letter.

"*Ques.*—Which is the Sabbath day?

"*Ans.*—Saturday is the Sabbath day.

"*Ques.*—Why do we observe Sunday instead of Saturday?

"*Ans.*—We observe Sunday instead of Saturday because the Catholic Church transferred the solemnity from Saturday to Sunday."—PETER GEIERMANN, *The Convert's Catechism of Catholic Doctrine* (1946 ed.), p. 50. Geiermann received the "apostolic blessing" of Pope Pius X on his labors, Jan. 25, 1910.

Do religious authorities acknowledge that there is no command in the Bible for the sanctification of Sunday?

Both Catholics and Protestant authorities acknowledge this fact. First we quote Catholic scholars:

NOTE—"You may read the Bible from Genesis to Revelation, and you will not find a single line authorizing the sanctification of Sunday. The Scriptures enforce the religious observance of Saturday, a day which we never sanctify."—JAMES CARDINAL GIBBONS, *The Faith of Our Fathers* (1917 ed.), pp. 72, 73.

"Nowhere in the Bible is it stated that worship should be changed from Saturday to Sunday. The fact is that the Church was in existence for several centuries before the Bible was given to the world. The Church made the Bible, the Bible did not make the Church.

"Now the Church . . . instituted, by God's authority, Sunday as the day of worship. This same Church, by the same divine authority, taught the doctrine of Purgatory long before the Bible was made. We have, therefore, the same authority for Purgatory as we have for Sunday."—MARTIN L. SCOTT, *Things Catholics Are Asked About* (1927 ed.), p. 136.

"If we consulted the Bible only, we should still have to keep holy the Sabbath Day, that is, Saturday."—JOHN LAUX, *A Course in Religion for Catholic High Schools and Academies,* vol. 1 (1936 ed.), p. 51. (Quoted by permission of Benziger Brothers, Inc., proprietors of the copyright.)

"For ages all Christian nations looked to the Catholic Church, and, as we have seen, the various states enforced by law her ordinances as to worship and cessation of Labor on Sunday. Protestantism, in discarding the authority of the church, has no good reason for its Sunday theory, and ought logically, to keep Saturday as the Sabbath.

"The Sunday, as a day of the week set apart for the obligatory public worship of Almighty God, to be sanctified by a suspension of all servile labor, trade, and worldly avocations and by exercises of devotion, *is purely a creation of the Catholic Church.*"—*The American Catholic Quarterly Review,* January 1883, pp. 152, 139.

"If Protestants would follow the Bible, they should worship God on the Sabbath Day. In keeping the Sunday they are following a law of the Catholic Church."—ALBERT SMITH, Chancellor of the Archdiocese of Baltimore, replying for the Cardinal in a letter of Feb. 10, 1920.

"Some theologians have held that God likewise directly determined the Sunday as the day of worship in the New Law, that He Himself has explicitly substituted the Sunday for the Sabbath. But this theory is now entirely abandoned. It is now commonly held that God simply gave His Church the power to set aside whatever day or days she would deem suitable as Holy Days. The Church chose Sunday, the first day of the week, and in the course of time added other days, as holy days."—VINCENT J. KELLY (Catholic), *Forbidden Sunday and Feast-Day Occupations* (1943 ed.), p. 2.

Do Protestant writers agree with this?

They do.

NOTE—"The Lord's day was merely of ecclesiastical institution. It was not introduced by virtue of the fourth commandment."—JEREMY TAYLOR (Church of England), *Ductor Dubitantium,* part 1, book 2, chap. 2, rule 6, secs. 51, 59 (1850 ed.), vol. 9, pp. 458, 464.

"The Lord's Day is not sanctified by any specific command or by any inevitable inference. In all the New Testament there is no hint or suggestion of a legal obligation binding any man, whether saint or sinner, to observe the Day. Its sanctity arises only out of what it means to the true believer."—J. J. TAYLOR (Baptist), *The Sabbatic Question,* p. 72.

"Because it was requisite to appoint a certain day, that the people might know when they ought to come together, it appears that the [Christian] Church did for that purpose appoint the Lord's day."—Augsburg Confession, part 2, art. 7, in PHILIP SCHAFF, *The Creeds of Christendom* (Harper), vol. 3, p. 69.

"And where are we told in the Scriptures that we are to keep the first day at all? We are commanded to keep the seventh; but we are nowhere commanded to keep the first day.

. . . The reason why we keep the first day of the week holy instead of the seventh is for the same reason that we observe many other things, not because the Bible, but because the church, has enjoined it."—ISAAC WILLIAMS (Anglican), *Plain Sermons on the Catechism,* vol. 1, pp. 334, 336.

"The Christian Church made no formal, but a gradual and almost unconscious, transference of the one day to the other."—F. W. Farrar, *The Voice From Sinai,* p. 167. This of itself is evidence that there was no divine command for the change of the Sabbath.

"They [the Catholics] allege the change of the Sabbath into the Lord's day, contrary, as it seemeth, to the Decalogue; and they have no example more in their mouths than the change of the Sabbath. They will needs have the Church's power to be very great, because it hath dispensed with a precept of the Decalogue."—*The Augsburg Confession* (Lutheran), part 2, art. 7, in PHILIP SCHAFF, *The Creeds of Christendom* (Scribners, 4th ed.), vol. 3, p. 64.

"It [the Roman Catholic Church] reversed the Fourth Commandment by doing away with the Sabbath of God's word, and instituting Sunday as a holiday."—N. SUMMERBELL, *History of the Christian Church* (1873), p. 415.

Good News About
GOD'S EVER- LASTING GRACE

THE PURPOSE OF THE LAW

What is the purpose of the law?

"By the deeds of the law there shall no flesh be justified in his sight: for *by the law is the knowledge of sin."* Romans 3:20.

How particular is God concerning Christian conduct?

"Whosoever shall keep the whole law, and yet offend in one point, he is guilty of all." James 2:10.

CHRIST SAVES MAN, MAGNIFIES LAW

What is the gospel declared to be?

"I am not ashamed of the gospel of Christ: for it is *the power of God unto salvation to every one that believeth."* Romans 1:16.

What is the significance of the name Jesus?

"Thou shalt call his name *Jesus:* for *he shall save his people from their sins."* Matthew 1:21.

In whom is this power to save from sin revealed?

"We preach . . . *Christ the power of God,* and the wisdom of God." 1 Corinthians 1:23, 24.

How was Christ's attitude toward God's law foretold?

"It is written of me, *I delight to do thy will, O my God: yea, thy law is within my heart."* Psalm 40:7, 8.

What does Christ promise of the new covenant?

"But now hath he obtained a more excellent ministry, by how much also he is the *mediator* of a better covenant." "For this is the covenant that I will make with the house of Israel after those days, saith the Lord; *I will put my laws into their mind, and write them in their hearts."* Hebrews 8:6, 10.

What must we do in order to benefit by Christ's work?

"With the heart man *believeth* unto righteousness; and with the mouth *confession* is made unto salvation." Romans 10:10.

For what did the apostle Paul trust Christ?

"I count all things but loss . . . that I may win Christ, and be found in him, not having mine own righteousness, which is of the law, but that which is through the faith of Christ, *the righteousness which is of God by faith."* Philippians 3:8, 9.

Does the faith which brings righteousness abolish the law?

"Do we then make void the law through faith? God forbid: yea, *we establish the law."* Romans 3:31.

NOTE—In the gospel, the law, first written in the heart of Christ, becomes "the law of the Spirit of life in Christ Jesus," and is thus transferred to the heart of the believer, where Christ dwells by faith. Thus the new covenant promise is fulfilled. This is righteousness by faith—a righteousness which is witnessed by the law, and revealed in the life in harmony with the law. Such faith, instead of making void the law, establishes it in the heart of the believer.

"The law demands obedience, but cannot produce it; it is holy in itself, but it cannot make us holy; it convinces of sin, but it cannot cure it; it reveals the disease, but it cannot provide the remedy; while the gospel both requires and enables, saves and sanctifies (Rom. 3:19-22; 4:15; 5:20, 21; 7:7-13; 2 Cor. 3:7-9; Gal. 3:21-24; 1 Tim. 1:8-11). . . .

"While it is in the very nature of all law to provoke opposition to itself in our wayward minds and wilful hearts, it is the essence of the gospel to appeal to the two strongest motives that actuate men and women—gratitude and love (contrast Rom. 7:5, 7-11; with 6:1-15; 2 Cor. 5:14, 15). . . .

"The gospel shows us the Saviour whom we need, and declares that he has fully obeyed the precepts of the law by his spotless life as our great representative, as well as completely exhausted its penalties through his atoning death as our great substitute (2 Cor. 5:21). . . . Divine justice and righteousness have been more entirely vindicated through his work for men than they could have been by the obedience or sufferings of the whole human race!

"It is the aim alike of the law and of the gospel to secure obedience, but the law compels us to it as a duty, making it irksome and distasteful, while the gospel constrains us to it as a privilege, rendering it easy and delightful. The law sets obedience before us as a means of salvation, and makes blessing strictly conditional upon it. The gospel reveals it as the natural consequence of redemption, and enjoins obedience as the necessary result of blessing."—WILLIAM C. PROCTER, *Moody Bible Institute Monthly* (copyrighted), November 1933, pp. 107, 108. Used by permission.

What did Christ take away?

"Behold the Lamb of God, which taketh away *the sin of the world."* John 1:29.

What has Christ abolished?

"Jesus Christ, who hath *abolished death,* and hath brought life and immortality to light through the gospel." 2 Timothy 1:10.

> NOTE—"Man . . . needs to be solemnly reminded that the law of the spirit of life in Christ sets him free from *the law of sin and death,* but not from the law of God."—G. CAMPBELL MORGAN, *The Ten Commandments* (Revell, 1901 ed.), p. 12.

What change is brought about through the gospel?

"But we all, with open face beholding as in a glass the glory of the Lord, are *changed into the same image* from glory to glory even as by the Spirit of the Lord." 2 Corinthians 3:18.

> NOTE—It is sometimes claimed that Christ changed, abolished, or took away the law, and put the gospel in its place; but this shows a misapprehension of the real work of Christ. The individual believer is changed by beholding the glory revealed in the gospel (2 Corinthians 4:4; John 1:14); death has been abolished through the death of Christ; and sin has been taken away by the great Sin Bearer, but the law of God still remains unchanged as the very foundation of His throne.

What spiritual interpretation did Christ give to the sixth and seventh commandments?

"Ye have heard that it was said by them of old time, Thou shalt not kill; and whosoever shall kill shall be in danger of the judgment: but I say unto you, *That whosoever is angry with his brother* without a cause shall be in danger of the judgment." Matthew 5:21, 22. "Ye have heard that it was said by them of old time, Thou shalt not commit adultery: but I say unto you, *That whosoever looketh on a woman to lust after her hath committed adultery with her already in his heart.*" Verses 27, 28.

Of what prophecy was this teaching a fulfillment?

"The Lord is well pleased for his righteousness' sake; *he will magnify the law, and make it honourable.*" Isaiah 42:21.

> NOTE—Christ not only gave a spiritual interpretation to the law, and Himself thus observed it, but He showed the holiness and the immutable nature of the law by dying on the cross to pay the penalty of its transgression. In this way, above all, He magnified the law.

GRACE AND THE LAW

In what promise was the gospel preached to Abraham?

"And the scripture . . . preached before the gospel unto Abraham, saying, *In thee shall all nations be blessed.*" Galatians 3:8.

On what basis was Abraham accounted righteous?

"For what saith the scripture? *Abraham believed God, and it was counted unto him for righteousness.*" Romans 4:3.

What scripture cuts off all hope of justification by works?

"By the deeds of the law there shall no flesh be justified in his sight: for by the law is the knowledge of sin." Romans 3:20.

In what way are all believers in Jesus justified?

"Being *justified freely by his grace* through the redemption that is in Christ Jesus." Verse 24.

Is the believer expected to go on in sin after this?

"What shall we say then? Shall we continue in sin, that grace may abound? God forbid. How shall we, that are dead to sin, live any longer therein?" Romans 6:1, 2.

What was Christ's personal attitude toward the law?

"Think not that I am come to destroy the law, or the prophets: *I am not come to destroy, but to fulfil.*" Matthew 5:17. "If ye keep my commandments, ye shall abide in my love; even as *I have kept my Father's commandments,* and abide in his love." John 15:10.

What scripture shows that God's remnant people will understand the proper relation between law and gospel?

"Here is the patience of the saints: *here are they that keep the commandments of God, and the faith of Jesus.*" Revelation 14:12.

> NOTE—"God has not left men enmeshed in their own disobedience—he has provided a way of restoration. This is not by pulling the heavenly standard down to the level of our guiltiness and weakness, but by lifting men up to the level of the eternal standard of his holiness. . . . This restoration is *restoration to a state of obedience to the Law.* . . . The atonement of Jesus Christ . . . bears an eternal relation to the Law of God, the Law which is holy, just and good. . . . [As the believer is] delivered by the work of Christ from the penalty of a broken law, and given a new heart by the Holy Spirit, by which he loves the way of obedience that once he shunned, the Law and the gospel are seen working in glorious harmony for the blessing of the redeemed man. To achieve this is *the one great purpose* of the proclamation of the gospel."—O. C. S. WALLACE, *What Baptists Believe,* pp. 83, 84. Copyright, 1934, by the Sunday School Board of the Southern Baptist Convention. Used by permission.

Good News About
BAPTISM

BELIEF, REPENTANCE, AND BAPTISM

What ordinance is closely associated with believing the gospel?

"And he said unto them, Go ye into all the world, and preach the gospel to every creature. he that believeth and is *baptized* shall be saved; but he that believeth not shall be damned." Mark 16:15, 16.

What did the apostle Peter associate with baptism in his instruction on the day of Pentecost?

"Then Peter said unto them, *Repent,* and be baptized every one of you in the name of Jesus Christ for the remission of sins." Acts 2:38.

In reply to his inquiry concerning salvation, what was the Philippian jailer told to do?

"And they said, *Believe on the Lord Jesus Christ,* and thou shalt be saved, and thy house." Acts 16:31.

What followed immediately after the jailer and his family had accepted Christ as their Saviour?

"And he took them [Paul and Silas] the same hour of the night, and washed their stripes; and was *baptized,* he and all his, straightway." Verse 33.

SPIRITUAL SIGNIFICANCE OF BAPTISM

In connection with Christian baptism, what is washed away?

"And now why tarriest thou? arise, and be baptized, and *wash away thy sins,* calling on the name of the Lord." Acts 22:16. (See Titus 3:5; 1 Peter 3:21.)

By what means are sins washed away?

"Unto him that loved us, and washed us from our sins *in his own blood.*" Revelation 1:5.

UNION WITH CHRIST IN BAPTISM

In whose name are believers to be baptized?

"Go ye therefore, and make disciples of all the nations, baptizing them into the name of the *Father* and of the *Son* and of the *Holy Ghost.*" Matthew 28:19, RV.

When believers are baptized into Christ, whom do they put on?

"For as many of you as have been baptized into Christ have *put on Christ.*" Galatians 3:27.

Into what experience are those baptized who are baptized into Christ?

"Know ye not, that so many of us as were baptized into Jesus Christ were *baptized into his death?*" Romans 6:3.

NOTE—Baptism is a gospel ordinance commemorating the *death, burial, and resurrection* of Christ. In baptism public testimony is given to the effect that the one baptized has been crucified with Christ, buried with Him, and is raised with Him to walk in newness of life. Only one mode of baptism can rightly represent these facts of experience, and that is immersion—the mode followed by Christ and the primitive church.

How is such a baptism described?

"Therefore we are *buried with him* by baptism into death: that like as Christ was raised up from the dead by the glory of the Father, even so we also should walk in newness of life." Verse 4.

How fully are we thus united with Christ in His experience of death and resurrection?

"For if we have been *planted together* in the likeness of his *death,* we shall be also in the likeness of *his resurrection.*" Verse 5.

What will follow this union with Christ?

"Now if we be dead with Christ, we believe that we shall also *live with him.*" Verse 8.

In what working of God is faith to be exercised in connection with baptism?

"Buried with him in baptism, wherein also ye are risen with him *through the faith of the operation of God, who hath raised him from the dead.*" Colossians 2:12.

BAPTISM AND THE HOLY SPIRIT

At the beginning of His ministry, what example did Jesus set for the benefit of His followers?

"Then cometh Jesus from Galilee to Jordan unto John, to be *baptized* of him." Matthew 3:13.

What occurred at the baptism of Jesus?

The Meaning of Baptism
Don Muth, Artist

"And Jesus, when he was baptized, went up straightway out of the water: and, lo, the heavens were opened unto him, and *he saw the Spirit of God descending like a dove, and lighting upon him:* and lo a voice from heaven, saying, *This is my beloved Son, in whom I am well pleased."* Verses 16, 17.

What promise is made to those who repent and are baptized?

"Then Peter said unto them, Repent, and be baptized every one of you in the name of Jesus Christ for the remission of sins, and *ye shall receive the gift of the Holy Ghost."* Acts 2:38.

What instruction did the apostle Peter give concerning the Gentiles who had believed?

"Can any man forbid water, that these should not be baptized, which have received the Holy Ghost as well as we? *And he commanded them to be baptized in the name of the Lord."* Acts 10:47, 48.

PHILIP BAPTIZES AN ETHIOPIAN AND SAMARITANS

What question did the eunuch ask after Philip had preached Jesus unto him?

"And as they went on their way, they came unto a certain water: and the eunuch said, See, here is water; *what doth hinder me to be baptized?"* Acts 8:36.

Where did Philip go to baptize the eunuch?

"And he commanded the chariot to stand still: and *they went down both into the water,* both Philip and the eunuch; and he baptized him." Verse 38.

How did the people of Samaria publicly testify to their faith in the preaching of Philip?

"But when they believed Philip preaching the things concerning the kingdom of God, and the name of Jesus Christ, *they were baptized,* both men and women." Verse 12.

UNITY AND HEAVENLY PURPOSE

How perfect is the unity into which believers are brought by being baptized into Christ?

"For as the body is one, and hath many members, and all the members of that one body, being many, are one body: so also is Christ. For by one Spirit are we all *baptized into one body,* whether we be Jews or Gentiles, whether we be bond or free; and have been all *made to drink into one Spirit."* 1 Corinthians 12:12, 13.

After being united with Christ in the likeness of His death and resurrection, what should the believer do?

"If ye then be risen with Christ, *seek those things which are above,* where Christ sitteth on the right hand of God." Colossians 3:1.

Good News About
DEATH

Of what was man formed in the beginning?

"God formed man *of the dust of the ground."* Genesis 2:7.

What act made him a living soul?

"And [God] *breathed into his nostrils the breath of life;* and man became a living soul." Same verse, last part.

NOTE—The living soul was not put *into* the man; but the breath of *life* which was put into man made *him*—the man, formed of the earth—a *living* soul, or creature. "Man became a living being," says the Smith-Goodspeed American translation. (University of Chicago Press.)

The Hebrew original translated "living soul" in this text is *nephesh chaiyah,* the same expression used in Genesis 1:24, translated "living creature."

The word *nephesh* occurs 755 times in the Hebrew Old Testament. In the King James Version the word is translated:

428 times as "soul." For example: Genesis 2:7; 12:5; Numbers 9:13; Psalm 6:3; Isaiah 1:14.

119 times, "life" (life's, lives). For example: Genesis 1:20, 30; 9:4; 1 Kings 19:14; Job 6:11; Psalm 38:12.

29 times, "person." For example: Numbers 31:19; 35:11, 15, 30; Deuteronomy 27:25; Joshua 20:3, 9; 1 Samuel 22:22.

15 times, "mind." For example: Deuteronomy 18:6; Jeremiah 15:1.

15 times, "heart." For example: Exodus 23:9; Proverbs 23:7.

9 times, "creature." Genesis 1:21, 24; 2:19; 9:10, 12, 15, 16; Leviticus 11:46.

7 times, "body" (or, dead body). Leviticus 21:11; Numbers 6:6; 9:6, 7, 10; 19:13; Haggai 2:13.

5 times, "dead." Leviticus 19:28; 21:1; 22:4; Numbers 5:2; 6:11.

3 times, "man." Exodus 12:16; 2 Kings 12:4; 1 Chronicles 5:21.

3 times, "me." Numbers 23:10; Judges 16:30; 1 Kings 20:32.

3 times, "beast." Leviticus 24:18.

2 times, "ghost." Job 11:20; Jeremiah 15:9.

1 time, "fish." Isaiah 19:10.

One or more times as various forms of the personal pronouns. (These figures are from Young's *Analytical Concordance.)*

Are other creatures besides man called "living souls"?

"And God created great whales, and every living creature that moveth, which the waters brought forth abundantly." Genesis 1:21. "And out of the ground the Lord God formed every beast of the field, and every fowl of the air; and brought them unto Adam to see what he would call them: and whatsoever Adam called every living creature, that was the name thereof." Genesis 2:19.

NOTE—Look up the nine instances of *nephesh,* "soul," translated as "creature," and you will see that they all refer to animals as "living creatures," or, as the words might have been translated, "living souls." On the phrase *nephesh chaiyah,* living soul or creature, in Genesis 1:24, Adam Clarke says: "A general term to express all creatures endued with animal life, in any of its infinitely varied gradations, from the half-reasoning *elephant* down to the stupid *potto,* or lower still, to the *polype,* which seems equally to share the vegetable and animal life."

An examination of the various occurrences of *nephesh* in the Old Testament shows that *nephesh* describes the individual rather than being a constituent part of the individual. It would be more correct, therefore, to say that a man *is* a *nephesh,* or "soul," than that he *has* a *nephesh,* or "soul." True, the expressions "my soul," "thy soul," "his soul," etc., occur frequently, but in most instances these are simply idiomatic expressions meaning "myself," "thyself," "himself," etc. Translators recognizing this have at times substituted the personal pronoun. For examples see Psalm 35:25; Proverbs 6:16; 16:26; Isaiah 5:14. In other instances *nephesh* means "life." Where such is its meaning "my soul" would mean "my life," "thy life," etc. See 2 Samuel 1:9; Jeremiah 4:30; etc.

In the New Testament the word translated "soul" is the Greek *psuchē.* This is the word which in the Septuagint, the Greek translation of the Hebrew Old Testament, translates the Hebrew word *nephesh.* New Testament writers used *psuchē* as the equivalent of *nephesh,* and did not attach to *psuchē* the pagan Greek concept of the allegedly immortal part of man as opposed to his body or perishable part. *Psuchē* is rendered by the following words in our King James Version:

58 times, "soul."

40 times, "life." For example: Mark 3:4; 10:45; Luke 6:9; 9:56; John 13:37; Romans 11:3; Revelation 8:9; 12:11.

3 times, "mind." Acts 14:2; Philippians 1:27; Hebrews 12:3.

1 time, "heart." Ephesians 6:6.

1 time, "heartily" (literally, "from the soul"). Colossians 3:23.

Psuchē is also used once in John 10:24 and in 2 Corinthians 12:15, in idiomatic phrases that are properly translated by the personal pronoun.

Do others besides man have the "breath of life"?

"And all flesh died that moved upon the earth, both of *fowl,* and of *cattle,* and of *beast,* and of *every creeping thing* that creepeth upon the earth, and every man: *all in whose nostrils was the breath of life."* Genesis 7:21, 22.

GOD'S ANSWERS TO YOUR QUESTIONS

When man gives up this spirit, what becomes of it?

"Then shall the dust return to the earth as it was: and *the spirit shall return unto God who gave it.*" Ecclesiastes 12:7.

NOTE—The word translated "breath" is *ruach,* which is defined in Gesenius' Lexicon as *"Rauch:*

(1) Spirit, breath. *(a)* Breath of the mouth. . . . Hence used of anything quickly perishing. . . . Often used of the vital spirit. . . . *(b)* Breath of the nostrils, snuffing, snorting. . . . Hence anger. . . . *(c)* Breath of air, air in motion, i.e., breeze. . . .

"(2) *Psuche anima,* breath, life, the vital principle, which shows itself in the breathing of the mouth and nostrils (see No.1, *a, b*), whether of men or of beast, Ecclesiastes 3:21; 8:8; 12:7; . . .

"(3) The rational mind or spirit. *(a)* As the seat of the senses, affections, and emotions of various kinds. . . . *(b)* As to the mode of thinking and acting. . . . *(c)* Of will and counsel. . . . More rarely *(d)* it is applied to the intellect. . . .

"(4) The Spirit of God."—TREGELLES' translation (1875 ed.).

The word *spirit* in the Old Testament is always from *ruach,* except twice (Job 26:4 and Proverbs 20:27 from *neshamah*). Ruach, besides being rendered 232 times as "spirit," is also translated:

90 times, "wind." ("Wind" in the Old Testament is always a translation of *ruach.*)

28 times, "breath." For example: Genesis 6:17; 7:15, 22; Job 12:10; Psalms 104:29; 146:4; Ecclesiastes 3:19.

8 times, "mind." Genesis 26:35; Proverbs 29:11; Ezekiel 11:5; 20:32; Daniel 5:20; Habakkuk 1:11.

4 times, "blast." Exodus 15:8; 2 Kings 19:7; Isaiah 25:4; 37:7.

Also translated one or more times by the following words: "anger," "air," "tempest," "vain."

At death the spirit goes back to the great Author of life. Having come from Him, it belongs to God, and man can have it eternally only as a gift from God, through Jesus Christ. (Romans 6:23.) When the spirit goes back to God, the dust, from which man's body is formed, goes back *as it was,* to the earth, and the individual no longer exists as a living, conscious, thinking being.

"Our personal identity is preserved in the resurrection, though not the same particles of matter or material substance as went into the grave. The wondrous works of God are a mystery to man. The spirit, the character of man, is returned to God, there to be preserved. In the resurrection every man will have his own character. God in his own time will call forth the dead, giving again the breath of life, and bidding the dry bones live. The same form will come forth, but it will be free of disease and every defect. It lives again bearing the same individuality of features, so that friend will recognize friend. There is no law of God in nature which shows that God gives back the same identical particles of matter which composed the body before death. God shall give the righteous dead a body that will please him."—E. G. WHITE, in *S.D.A. Bible Commentary,* vol. 6, p. 1093.

FROM WRATH AND DEATH TO LIFE

Who only have hold of the life eternal?

"He that hath the Son hath life; and he that hath not the Son of God hath not life." 1 John 5:12.

NOTE—The veriest sinner has this temporal life; but when he yields up this life, he has no prospect or promise of the life eternal. That can be received only through Christ.

Why was Adam driven from Eden and the tree of life?

"And now, lest he put forth his hand, and take also of the tree of life, and eat, and *live for ever.*" Genesis 3:22.

What was done to keep man away from the tree of life?

"So he drove out the man; and he placed at the east of the garden of Eden Cherubims, and a flaming sword which turned every way, to keep the way of the tree of life." Verse 24.

How are all men in the natural state regarded?

"We all . . . were by nature *the children of wrath,* even as others." Ephesians 2:3.

If the wrath of God abides on us, of what are we deprived?

"He that believeth not the Son *shall not see life;* but the wrath of God abideth on him." John 3:36.

Through whom can we be saved from wrath and given immortality?

"Much more then, being now justified by his blood, we shall be saved from wrath through him." Romans 5:9. *"Our Saviour Jesus Christ, who hath abolished death, and hath brought life and immortality to light through the gospel."* 2 Timothy 1:10.

Who only possesses inherent immortality?

"The blessed and only Potentate, the King of kings, and Lord of lords; *who only hath immortality.*" 1 Timothy 6:15, 16.

NOTE—This word for immortality as applied to God is not *aphtharsia,* "incorruptibility," which is used twice, 2 Timothy 1:10 and Romans 2:7, but *athanasia,* "deathlessness," which is used also in 1 Corinthians 15:53, 54. God is the only being who possesses original life or immortality in Himself. All others must receive it from God. (See John 5:26; 6:27; 10:10, 27, 28; Romans 6:23; 1 John 5:11.)

To whom is eternal life promised?

"To them who by patient continuance in well doing *seek for glory and honour and immortality,* eternal life." Romans 2:7.

NOTE—One does not need to seek for a thing which he already possesses. The fact that we are to seek for immortality is proof in itself that we do not now possess it.

Again, it would mar the felicity of one's employment in heaven could he look upon earth and see his friends and relatives suffering from persecution, want, cold, or hunger, or sorrowing for the dead. God's way is best—that all sentient

58

life, animation, activity, thought, and consciousness should cease at death, and all should wait till the resurrection for their eternal reward. (See Hebrews 11:39, 40.)

When will the faithful be changed to immortality?
"We shall not all sleep, but *we shall all be changed,* in a moment, in the twinkling of an eye, *at the last trump:* for the trumpet shall sound, and the dead shall be raised incorruptible, and we shall be changed." 1 Corinthians 15:51, 52.

What is then to be swallowed up?
"So when this corruptible shall have put on incorruption, and this mortal shall have put on immortality, then shall be brought to pass the saying that is written, *Death is swallowed up in victory."* Verse 54. (See verse 57.)

NOTE—Isaiah 25:8 says, "He will swallow up death in victory; and the Lord God will wipe away tears from off all faces; and the rebuke of his people shall he take away from off all the earth: for the Lord hath spoken it." When Christ comes in the clouds of heaven, the amazing transformation from mortal to immortal takes place, both of the righteous dead and the righteous living. Then regenerated man is completely saved beyond all possibilities of death and will be no longer troubled with this great enemy.

What is the wages of sin?
"The wages of sin is *death."* Romans 6:23.

Through whom only is there salvation from sin?
"Neither is there salvation in any other: for there is none other name under heaven given among men, whereby we must be saved." Acts 4:12.

Why did God give His only-begotten Son?
"That whosoever believeth in him should not *perish,* but have *everlasting life."* John 3:16.

What does Christ declare Himself to be?
"I am the way, the truth, and *the life."* John 14:6.

What does He give to those who follow Him?
"My sheep hear my voice, and I know them, and they follow me: and *I give unto them eternal life;* and they shall never perish, neither shall any man pluck them out of my hand." John 10:27, 28.

In whom is the life eternal?
"And this is the record, that God hath given to us eternal life, *and this life is in his Son."* 1 John 5:11.

Who only have this life?
"He that hath the Son hath life; and he that hath not the Son of God hath not life." Verse 12. *"He that heareth my word and believeth on him that sent me, hath everlasting life,* and shall not come into condemnation; but is passed from death unto life." John 5:24.

WHAT DEATH IS LIKE

By what figure does the Bible represent death?
"But I would not have you to be ignorant, brethren, concerning them which are *asleep,* that ye sorrow not, even as others which have no hope." 1 Thessalonians 4:13. (See also 1 Corinthians 15:18, 20; John 11:11-14.)

NOTE—In sound sleep one is wholly lost to consciousness; time goes by unmeasured; and mental activity is suspended for the time being.

Where does Daniel represent the dead as sleeping?
"And many of them that *sleep in the dust of the earth* shall awake." Daniel 12:2. (See also Ecclesiastes 3:20; 9:10.)

What does one in this condition know about his family?
"His sons come to honour, and *he knoweth it not;* and they are brought low, but *he perceiveth it not of them."* Job 14:21.

What becomes of man's thoughts at death?
"His breath goeth forth, he returneth to his earth; *in that very day his thoughts perish."* Psalm 146:4.

Do the dead know "anything"?
"For the living know that they shall die: *but the dead know not any thing."* Ecclesiastes 9:5.

Do they take any part in earthly things?
"Also their *love,* and their *hatred,* and their *envy,* is now *perished; neither have they any more a portion for ever in any thing that is done under the sun."* Verse 6.

NOTE—If one remained conscious after death, he would know of the promotion or dishonor of his sons; but in death one loses all the attributes of mind—love, hatred, envy, etc. Thus it is plain that his thoughts have perished, and that he can have nothing more to do with the things of this world. But if, as taught by some, man's powers of thought continue after death, he lives; and if he lives, he must be somewhere. Where is he? Is he in heaven or hell? If he goes to either place at death, what then is the need of a future judgment, or of a resurrection, or of the second coming of Christ? If men go to their reward at death, before the judgment takes place, then their rewards precede their awards.

How much does one know of God when dead?
"For in death *there is no remembrance of thee."* Psalm 6:5.

NOTE—As already seen, the Bible everywhere represents the dead as *asleep,* with not even a remembrance of God. If they were in heaven or hell, would Jesus have said, "Our friend Lazarus *sleepeth"?* John 11:11. If so, calling him to life was really robbing him of the bliss of heaven that rightly belonged to him. The parable of the rich man and Lazarus (Luke 16) teaches not consciousness in death, but that riches will avail nothing in the judgment and that poverty will not keep one out of heaven.

WHERE ARE THE DEAD?

Are not the righteous dead in heaven praising God?

"For *David is not ascended into the heavens."* Acts 2:34. *"The dead praise not the Lord,* neither any that go down into silence." Psalm 115:17.

Where did Job say he would await his final change?

"If a man die, shall he live again? all the days of my appointed time will I wait, *till my change* come." Job 14:14. *"If I wait, the grave is mine house:* I have made my bed in the darkness." Job 17:13.

> NOTE—The Hebrew original for "grave" in this verse is *she'ol,* meaning among other things a dark, hollow, subterranean place, used simply in reference to the abode of the dead in general, without distinguishing between the good and the bad. *(Young's Analytical Concordance.)*
>
> The same word is also translated "pit" 3 times (Numbers 16:30, 33; Job 17:16), and "hell" 31 times (every occurrence of the word "hell" in the Authorized Version of the Old Testament). The translation of *she'ol* as "grave" 31 times bears witness to the unsuitability of the present English word *hell* to the idea of *she'ol,* especially in reference to Jacob (Genesis 37:35; 42:38), Job (Job 14:13), David (Psalm 30:3), and even Christ (Psalm 16:10; cf. Acts 2:27, 31). The American Revised Version avoids choosing between "hell" and "grave" by retaining *she'ol* as an untranslated place name, just as it does the corresponding Greek word *hadēs* in the New Testament. It should be remembered that "hell" in the Old Testament always means *she'ol,* a place of darkness and silence, not a place of fiery torment.

WHEN THE DEAD RISE AGAIN

What must take place before the dead can praise God?

"Thy dead men shall live, together with my dead body shall they arise. *Awake and sing, ye that dwell in dust:* for . . . the earth shall cast out the dead." Isaiah 26:19.

When did the psalmist say he would be satisfied?

"As for me, I will behold thy face in righteousness: I shall be satisfied, *when I awake, with thy likeness."* Psalm 17:15.

Were there to be no resurrection of the dead, what would be the condition of those fallen asleep in Christ?

"For if the dead rise not, then is not Christ raised. . . . *Then they also which are fallen asleep in Christ are perished."* 1 Corinthians 15:16-18.

When will be the resurrection of the righteous?

"For the Lord himself shall descend from heaven with a shout, with the voice of the archangel, and with the trump of God: *and the dead in Christ shall rise first."* 1 Thessalonians 4:16.

> NOTE—If, as stated in Ecclesiastes 9:5, the dead know not anything, then they have no knowledge of the lapse of time; it will seem to them when they awake that absolutely no time has elapsed. "Six thousand years in the grave to a dead man is no more than a wink of the eye to the living." And herein lies a most comforting thought in the Bible doctrine of the sleep of the dead. To those who sleep in Jesus, their sleep, whether one year, 1,000 years, or 6,000 years, will be but as if the moment of sad parting were followed instantly by the glad reunion in the presence of Jesus at His glorious appearing and the resurrection of the just.
>
> It ought also to be a comforting thought to those whose lives have been filled with anxiety and grief for deceased loved ones who persisted in sin, to know that they are not now suffering in torments, but, with all the rest of the dead, are quietly sleeping in their graves.

Good News About
HELL

What question does the apostle Peter ask regarding the wicked?

"What shall the end be of them that obey not the gospel of God?" 1 Peter 4:17.

What does the Bible say is the wages of sin? What is to be the fate of one who persists in sin?

"For *the wages of sin is death."* Romans 6:23. "The soul that sinneth, it shall *die."* Ezekiel 18:4.

COMPLETENESS OF THE DESTRUCTION

What will be the character of this death?

"Who shall be punished with *everlasting destruction."* 2 Thessalonians 1:9.

What will befall those who do not repent?

"Except ye repent, ye shall all likewise *perish."* Luke 13:3. "But these, as natural brute beasts, made to be taken and destroyed, speak evil of the things that they understand not; and *shall utterly perish in their own corruption."* 2 Peter 2:12.

How does John the Baptist describe the destruction of the wicked?

"He will . . . gather his wheat into the garner; *but he will burn up the chaff with unquenchable fire."* Matthew 3:12.

For whom was this fire originally prepared?

"Then shall he say also unto them on the left hand, Depart from me, ye cursed, into everlasting fire, *prepared for the devil and his angels."* Matthew 25:41.

NOTE—This fire is called "everlasting" (Greek, *aiōnion,* "age lasting") because of the character of the work it does; just as it is called "unquenchable" (Greek, *asbestos,* "unquenchable," "unquenched") because it cannot be put out, and not because it will not go out when it has done its work. "Eternal fire" reduced Sodom and Gomorrah to ashes. (Jude 7; 2 Peter 2:6.)

Will any part of the wicked be left?

"For, behold, the day cometh, that shall burn as an oven; and all the proud, yea, and *all* that do wickedly, shall be stubble: and the day that cometh shall *burn them up,* saith the Lord of hosts, *that it shall leave them neither root nor branch."* Malachi 4:1.

How completely will man be destroyed in hell?

"Fear him which is able to *destroy both soul and body in hell."* Matthew 10:28.

NOTE—This scripture proves that the soul is neither immortal nor indestructible.

The everlasting punishment—"destruction"—of the wicked is this destruction of soul and body in hell (Greek, *Geenna* [Gehenna]).

"Hell" in the New Testament is translated from three Greek words:

Hadēs, 10 times. Matthew 11:23; 16:18; Luke 10:15; 16:23; Acts 2:27, 31; Revelation 1:18; 6:8; 20:13, 14. *(Hadēs* is also "grave" once, 1 Corinthians 15:55.)

Geenna (Gehenna), 12 times. Matthew 5:22, 29, 30; 10:28; 18:9; 23:15, 33; Mark 9:43, 45, 47; Luke 12:5; James 3:6.

Tartaroō, 1 time (the only occurrence in the Bible). 2 Peter 2:4.

Hadēs (the lower world, place of the dead, the grave) is the equivalent of *she'ol.* It is used in Acts 2:27, 31, to translate from Psalm 16:10. *Tartaroō,* describing the fall of Satan's rebel angels, is a verb, meaning "to cast down to Tartarus." This is a striking figure of speech, alluding to the Tartarus of Greek mythology, an abyss deeper than Hades, the prison of the Titans, who fought against the gods.

Gehenna, the only other word for hell, is the Valley of Hinnom, used symbolically of the fires of the last great day of judgment. This is the word that is used in Matthew 10:28 to describe the place where the wicked will be destroyed body and soul.

WHERE, WHEN, AND HOW

When will the wicked be punished?

"But the heavens and the earth, which are now, by the same word are kept in store, *reserved unto fire against the day of judgment and perdition of ungodly men."* 2 Peter 3:7.

NOTE—The present heavens and earth and sinners await the fires of the last day. The Greek for "perdition" is *apoleia,* "loss," "destruction."

What will be the result of the fires of the last day?

"Looking for and hasting unto the coming of the day of God, wherein *the heavens being on fire shall be dissolved, and the elements shall melt with fervent heat."* "The earth also and the works that are therein shall be burned up." Verses 12, 10.

How does Christ say sin and sinners will be eliminated?

"His angels . . . *shall gather out of his kingdom all things that offend, and them which do iniquity; and shall cast them into a furnace of fire."* Matthew 13:41, 42.

When are the wicked dead to be raised to receive this final punishment?

"But the rest of the dead lived not again *until the thousand years were finished."* Revelation 20:5.

Whence will come the fire that will destroy them?

"And they went up on the breadth of the earth, and compassed the camp of the saints about, and the beloved city: *and fire came down from God out of heaven, and devoured them."* Verse 9.

NOTE—This is called God's "strange act" and His "strange work"—the work of destruction. (Isaiah 28:21.) But by this means God will once and forever cleanse the universe of sin and all its sad results. Death itself will then be at an end—cast into the lake of fire. (Revelation 20:14.)

By what figure does Malachi describe the destruction of the wicked?

"And ye shall tread down the wicked; for *they shall be ashes under the soles of your feet."* Malachi 4:3.

NOTE—The wicked are to be utterly destroyed—consumed away into smoke, brought to ashes. Through sin they have forfeited the right to life and an immortal existence, and chosen the way of death and destruction. By their choice they have proved themselves worthless, like chaff, briers, thorns, etc. They will themselves have lost their opportunity to obtain eternal life, by the way in which they used their probationary time. Their destruction will, in fact, be an act of love and mercy on the part of God; for to perpetuate their lives would only be to perpetuate sin, sorrow, suffering, and misery. Terrible, therefore, as this judgment will be, there will, in consequence of it, be nothing of value lost—nothing lost worth saving. The experience of sin will be over, and God's original plan of peopling the earth with a race of holy, happy beings will be carried out. (2 Peter 3:13.)

What is this final destruction of the wicked called?

"This is *the second death."* Revelation 20:14.

After the burning day, what will appear?

"We, according to his promise, look for *new heavens and a new earth,* wherein dwelleth righteousness." 2 Peter 3:13.

How will the righteous be recompensed in the earth?

"Blessed are the meek: for *they shall inherit the earth."* Matthew 5:5. "Then shall the righteous shine forth as the sun *in the kingdom of their Father."* Matthew 13:43.

NOTE—Satan and the wicked now have this world as their "place." In due time Christ will have it. He will cleanse it from sin and sinners, and restore it, that He may give it to the saints of the Most High for an everlasting possession. (See Daniel 7:18, 22, 27.)

Good News About
A THOUSAND YEARS OF PEACE

THE MILLENNIUM AND JUDGMENT

What text definitely brings the millennium to view?

"And I saw thrones, and they sat upon them, and *judgment was given unto them: . . . and they lived and reigned with Christ a thousand years.*" Revelation 20:4.

Whom does Paul say the saints are to judge?

"Dare any of you, having a matter against another, go to law before the unjust, and not before the saints? *Do ye not know that the saints shall judge the world? . . . Know ye not that we shall judge angels?*" 1 Corinthians 6:1-3.

> NOTE—From these scriptures it is plain that the saints of all ages are to be engaged with Christ in a work of "judgment" during the millennium, or the period of one thousand years.

THE MILLENNIUM BEGINS

How many resurrections are there to be?

"Marvel not at this: for the hour is coming, in the which all that are in the graves shall hear his voice, and shall come forth; they that have done good, unto *the resurrection of life;* and they that have done evil, unto *the resurrection of damnation.*" John 5:28, 29.

What class only have part in the first resurrection?

"*Blessed and holy* is he that hath part in the first resurrection: on such the second death hath no power." Revelation 20:6.

What will Christ do with the saints when He comes?

"I will come again, and *receive you unto myself; that where I am, there ye may be also.*" John 14:3.

> NOTE—In other words, Christ will take them to heaven, there to live and reign with Him during the one thousand years.

Where did John, in vision, see the saints?

"After this I beheld, and, lo, a great multitude, which no man could number, of all nations, and kindreds, and people, and tongues, *stood before the throne, and before the Lamb,* clothed with white robes, and palms in their hands." Revelation 7:9.

> NOTE—This scripture shows plainly that the righteous

are all taken to heaven immediately after the first resurrection. This accords with the words of Christ in John 14:1-3, where He says, "I go to prepare a place for you. And if I go and prepare a place for you, I will come again, and *receive you unto myself; that where I am, there ye may be also.*" Peter desired to accompany Christ to those mansions; but Jesus answered, "Thou canst not follow me now; *but thou shalt follow me afterwards.*" John 13:36. This makes it clear that when Christ returns to earth to receive His people, He takes them to the Father's house in heaven.

What becomes of the living wicked when Christ comes?

"*As it was in the days of Noe,* so shall it be also in the days of the Son of man. They did eat, they drank, they married wives, they were given in marriage, until the day that Noe entered into the ark, and *the flood came, and destroyed them all. Likewise also as it was in the days of Lot; . . .* the same day that Lot went out of Sodom it rained fire and brimstone from heaven, and destroyed them all. *Even thus shall it be in the day when the Son of man is revealed.*" Luke 17:26-30.

What does the apostle Paul say concerning this?

"When they shall say, Peace and safety; *then sudden destruction cometh upon them, . . . and they shall not escape.*" 1 Thessalonians 5:3.

> NOTE—When Christ comes, the righteous will be delivered and taken to heaven, and all the living wicked will be suddenly destroyed, as they were at the time of the Flood. For further proof see 2 Thessalonians 1:7-9; Revelation 6:14-17; 19:11-21; Jeremiah 25:30-33. There will be no general resurrection of the wicked until the end of the one thousand years. This will leave the earth desolate and without human inhabitant during this period.

How long is Satan to be imprisoned on this earth?

"I saw an angel come down from heaven, having the key of the bottomless pit and a great chain in his hand. And he laid hold on the dragon, that old serpent, which is the Devil, and Satan, and *bound him a thousand years,* and cast him into the bottomless pit, and shut him up, and set a seal upon him, that he should deceive the nations no more, till the thousand years should be fulfilled." Revelation 20:1-3.

> NOTE—The word rendered "bottomless pit" in this text is *abussos,* the Greek term employed by the Septuagint in Genesis 1:2, as the equivalent of the Hebrew word rendered "deep" in our English versions. A more literal translation would be "abyss." It is a term applied to the earth in its des-

olate, waste, chaotic, dark, uninhabited condition. In this condition it will remain during the one thousand years. It will be the dreary prison house of Satan during this period. Here, in the midst of the moldering bones of wicked dead, slain at Christ's coming, the broken-down cities, and the wreck and ruin of all the pomp and power of this world, Satan will have opportunity to reflect upon the results of his rebellion against God.

CLOSE OF THE MILLENNIUM

The righteous dead are raised at Christ's second coming. When will the rest of the dead, the wicked, be raised?

"The rest of the dead lived not again *until the thousand years were finished.*" Revelation 20:5.

NOTE—From this we see that the beginning and the close of the millennium, or one thousand years, are marked by the two resurrections.

The word *millennium* is from two Latin words, *mille,* meaning a "thousand," and *annus,* "year"—a thousand years. It covers the time during which Satan is to be bound and wicked men and angels are to be judged. This period is bounded by distinct events. Its beginning is marked by the close of probation, the pouring out of the seven last plagues, the second coming of Christ, and the resurrection of the righteous dead. It closes with the resurrection of the wicked, and their final destruction in the lake of fire. (See diagram.)

What change is made in Satan's condition at the close of the one thousand years?

"After that *he must be loosed a little season.*" Verse 3.

NOTE—At the close of the one thousand years, Christ, accompanied by the saints, comes to the earth again, to execute judgment upon the wicked, and to prepare the earth, by a re-creation, for the eternal abode of the righteous. At this time, in answer to the summons of Christ, the wicked dead of all ages awake to life. This is the second resurrection, the resurrection unto damnation. The wicked come forth with the same rebellious spirit which possessed them in this life. Then Satan is loosed from his long period of captivity and inactivity.

As soon as the wicked are raised, what does Satan at once proceed to do?

"When the thousand years are expired, Satan shall be loosed out of his prison, and shall go out to *deceive the nations* which are in the four quarters of the earth, Gog and Magog, *to gather them together to battle:* the number of whom is as the sand of the sea." Verses 7, 8.

Against whom do the wicked go to make war, and what is the outcome?

"They went up on the breadth of the earth, and *compassed the camp of the saints about, and the beloved city;* and *fire came down from God out of heaven, and devoured them.*" Verse 9.

NOTE—This is the last act in the great controversy between Christ and Satan. The whole human race meet here for the first and last time. The eternal separation of the righteous from the wicked here takes place. At this time the judgment of God is executed upon the wicked in the lake of fire. This is the second death. This ends the great rebellion against God and His government. Now is heard the voice of God as He sits upon his throne, speaking to the saints, and

1. END OF SEVEN LAST PLAGUES
2. CHRIST'S SECOND COMING
3. RIGHTEOUS DEAD RAISED
4. WICKED PERISH--SATAN BOUND
5. RIGHTEOUS ASCEND TO HEAVEN

THE MIL
1,000 YEARS B

FIRST RESURRECTION

THE END OF THE WORLD

EARTH DESOLATE

saying, "Behold, I make all things new"; and out of the burning ruins of the old earth there springs forth before the admiring gaze of the millions of the redeemed "a new heaven and a new earth," in which they shall find an everlasting inheritance and dwelling place.

CONDITIONS DURING THE MILLENNIUM

What description does the prophet Jeremiah give of the earth during this time?

"I beheld the earth, and, lo, it was *without form, and void;* and the heavens, and they had no light. I beheld the mountains, and, lo, they trembled, and all the hills moved lightly. I beheld, and, lo, *there was no man,* and all the birds of the heavens were fled. I beheld, and, lo, *the fruitful place was a wilderness, and all the cities thereof were broken down* at the presence of the Lord, and by his fierce anger." Jeremiah 4:23-26.

NOTE—At the coming of Christ the earth is reduced to a chaotic state—to a mass of ruins. The heavens depart as a scroll when it is rolled together; mountains are moved out of their places; and the earth is left a dark, dreary, desolate waste. (See Isaiah 24:1-3; Revelation 6:14-17.)

How does Isaiah speak of the wicked at this time?

"It shall come to pass in that day, that the Lord shall punish the host of the high ones that are on high, and the kings of the earth upon the earth. And they shall be gathered together, as prisoners are gathered in the pit, and *shall be shut up in prison,* and after many days shall they be visited." Isaiah 24:21, 22.

NOTE—The millennium is a great sabbath of rest, both for the earth and for God's people. For six thousand years the earth and its inhabitants have been groaning under the curse of sin. The millennium, the seventh thousand, will be a sabbath of rest and release; for, says the prophet concerning the land, "as long as she lay desolate she kept *sabbath."* 2 Chronicles 36:21. "There remaineth therefore a rest [margin, *"keeping of a sabbath"]* to the people of God." Hebrews 4:9. This precedes the new-earth state.

The millennium is the closing period of God's great week of time—a great sabbath of rest to the earth and to the people of God.

It follows the close of the gospel age, and precedes the setting up of the everlasting kingdom of God on earth.

It comprehends what in the Scriptures is frequently spoken of as "the day of the Lord."

It is bounded at each end by a resurrection.

Its beginning is marked by the pouring out of the seven last plagues, the second coming of Christ, the resurrection of the righteous dead, the binding of Satan, and the translation of the saints to heaven; and its close, by the descent of the New Jerusalem, with Christ and the saints, from heaven, the resurrection of the wicked dead, the loosing of Satan, and the final destruction of the wicked.

During the one thousand years the earth lies desolate; Satan and his angels are confined here; and the saints, with Christ, sit in judgment on the wicked, preparatory to their final punishment.

The wicked dead are then raised; Satan is loosed for a little season, and he and the host of the wicked encompass the camp of the saints and the Holy City, when fire comes down from God out of heaven and devours them. The earth is cleansed by the same fire that destroys the wicked, and, renewed, becomes the eternal abode of the saints.

The millennium is part of "the age to come." Its close will mark the beginning of the new-earth state.

1. CHRIST AND SAINTS DESCEND
2. HOLY CITY DESCENDS
3. WICKED DEAD RAISED
4. SATAN LOOSED
5. WICKED DESTROYED

Joe Malmede, Artist

SECOND RESURRECTION

FOR 1,000 YEARS   NEW EARTH AND ETERNITY

Good News About
THE JUDGMENT

(THE 2300 DAYS OF DANIEL 8, 9)

What startling message is given in Revelation 14:7?

"Fear God, and give glory to him; for the *hour of his judgment is come:* and worship him that made heaven, and earth, and the sea, and the fountains of waters."

When is the hour of God's judgment according to the message given to Daniel?

"He said unto me, Unto two thousand and three hundred days; then shall the sanctuary be cleansed." Daniel 8:14.

NOTE—By the study of the succeeding chapters on the sanctuary, it will be seen that the cleansing of the sanctuary is the work of judgment. The Jewish people understood it so. This 2300-day period, being 2300 literal years (Ezekiel 4:6), reaches down to the cleansing of the sanctuary in heaven, or, in other words, to the time when the investigative judgment begins, as described in Daniel 7:9, 10.

Why was not this time period fully explained when the angel first appeared to Daniel?

"I Daniel fainted, and was *sick certain days;* afterward I rose up, and did the king's business; and I was astonished at the vision, but none understood it." Daniel 8:27.

NOTE—The prophet had been given a vision of the great nations of his and succeeding days and the persecutions of God's people, concluding with the time period pointing to the cleansing of the sanctuary. But the aged Daniel fainted and was sick certain days. Consequently, the interpretation was arrested, and was not completed until after the recovery of the prophet. The vision and its partial explanation were given in the third year of Belshazzar's reign with his father, Nabonidus; the interpretation of the time period was given following the fall of Babylon, in the first year of Darius.

At some time subsequent to Daniel's recovery from his illness, to what did he turn his attention?

"In the first year of Darius . . . I Daniel understood by books the number of the years, whereof the word of the Lord came to Jeremiah the prophet, that he would accomplish seventy years in the desolations of Jerusalem." Daniel 9:1, 2.

NOTE—Nebuchadnezzar besieged Jerusalem in the third year of Jehoiakim (Daniel 1:1), and Jeremiah announced the seventy-year captivity in the fourth year of Jehoiakim (Jeremiah 25:1, 12). This means that the first deportation of the Jews to Babylon, when Daniel and his com-

panions were carried away, was at that time. The seventy years of Jeremiah's prophecy would expire in 536 B.C. Since the first year of the Persian Empire began in 538 B.C., the restoration period was therefore only two years distant from that time.

What did this nearness of the time of restoration from captivity lead Daniel to do?

"I set my face unto the Lord God, to seek by *prayer and supplications,* with fasting, and sackcloth, and ashes." Daniel 9:3.

In what especially was the prophet interested?

"Now therefore, O our God, hear the prayer of thy servant, and his supplications, and cause thy face to shine upon thy *sanctuary that is desolate,* for the Lord's sake." Verse 17.

GABRIEL AGAIN APPEARS

While Daniel was praying concerning the sanctuary lying desolate at Jerusalem, who appeared on the scene?

"Yea, whiles I was speaking in prayer, even the man *Gabriel,* whom I had seen in the vision at the beginning, being caused to fly swiftly, touched me about the time of the evening oblation." Verse 21.

NOTE—It was fitting that the angel Gabriel should return to the prophet for the purpose of explaining that portion of the prophecy in Daniel 8 which had not been interpreted, the time period, when Daniel was earnestly praying for the sanctuary made desolate at Jerusalem. The angel not only would open to his vision the earthly typical sanctuary and its future, but would give him, for the benefit of those living at the time of the end, a view of the true heavenly service.

What did the angel at once ask the prophet to consider?

"He informed me, and talked with me, and said, O Daniel, I am now come forth to give thee skill and understanding. . . . Therefore understand the matter, and *consider the vision."* Daniel 9:22, 23.

NOTE—It is evident that the angel began just where he had left off in explanation of the prophecy of the eighth chapter; for he introduces no new line of prophecy, no new vision. "Consider *the* vision." In the Hebrew the definite article *the* here clearly specifies the vision previously mentioned. This is obviously the vision of the preceding chapter. Since the 2300-day period was the only part of the former vision left unexplained, the angel would naturally begin with an interpretation of that period.

What portion of the 2300 days mentioned in the vision was allotted to the Jews?

"Seventy weeks [literally, *"seventy sevens"]* are determined upon thy people and upon thy holy city." Verse 24.

NOTE—The word translated "weeks," literally, "sevens," is used in Jewish literature to refer to periods of seven days and also to periods of seven years. Jewish and Christian scholars, generally, have concluded that the context here requires that "weeks" of years be understood. "Seventy weeks" of seven years each would be 490 years.

In postbiblical Hebrew the word here translated "determined" had the meaning "to cut," "to cut off," "to determine," "to decree." In view of the fact that the seventy weeks of Daniel 9 are a part of the 2300 days of chapter 8, and were cut off from them and assigned particularly to the Jews, the meaning "to cut" here seems especialiy appropriate.

The seventy weeks, therefore, were "determined," or cut off. There are two periods of time under consideration: the first, the 2300-day period; the second, the seventy-week period. They both had to do with the restoration of the Jewish people and the sanctuary, for the Jews were in captivity and the sanctuary was in ruins. The two periods must then begin with the restoration, and at the same time. The full restoration of the Jewish laws and government pertaining to the people and their sanctuary took place in 457 B.C., as we shall see later. It is reasonable, then, to say that the seventy weeks were a part of the 2300-year period, and that they were thus "cut off" as a period pertaining to the Jewish people and their sanctuary service.

What was to be accomplished at or near the close of this seventy-week period?

"To finish the transgression, and to make an end of sins, and to make reconciliation for iniquity, and to bring in everlasting righteousness, and to seal up the vision and prophecy, and to anoint the most Holy." Verse 24.

NOTE—*"To Finish the Transgression."*—The Jews were to fill up the measure of their iniquity by rejecting and crucifying the Messiah; they would then no longer be His peculiar, chosen people. Read Matthew 21:38-43; 23:32-38; 27:25.

"To Make an End of Sins."—The best explanation of this clause is given in Hebrews 9:26: "Now once in the end of the world hath he appeared to put away sin by the sacrifice of himself"; and in Romans 8:3: "What the law could not do, in that it was weak through the flesh, God sending his own Son in the likeness of sinful flesh, and for sin, condemned sin in the flesh."

"To Bring in Everlasting Righteousness."—This must mean the righteousness of Christ—that righteousness by which He was enabled to make an atonement for sin, and which, through faith, may be imputed to the penitent believer.

"To Anoint the Most Holy."—The Hebrew words here used are regularly employed of the sanctuary, but not of persons. The anointing of the "most Holy," then, must refer to the anointing of the heavenly sanctuary, when Christ became the "minister of the sanctuary, and of the true tabernacle, which the Lord pitched, and not man." Hebrews 8:2.

THE BEGINNING OF THE TIME PERIOD

When did the angel say that the seventy weeks were to begin?

"Know therefore and understand, that from the going forth of the commandment to restore and to build Jerusalem unto the Messiah the Prince shall be seven weeks, and threescore and two weeks: the street shall be built again, and the wall, even in troublous times." Daniel 9:25.

NOTE—Seventy weeks would be a period of 490 literal years. Sixty-nine (seven weeks and sixty-two weeks) of the seventy weeks were to reach "unto the Messiah the Prince." *Messiah* is Christ, "the Anointed." *Messiah* is the Hebrew word, and *Christ* the Greek word, meaning "anointed."

How was Jesus anointed?

"God anointed Jesus of Nazareth with the Holy Ghost and with power." Acts 10:38.

At what time did Jesus receive the special anointing of the Holy Spirit?

"Jesus also being baptized, and praying, the heaven was opened, and the Holy Ghost descended in a bodily shape like a dove upon him, and a voice came from heaven, which said, Thou art my beloved Son." Luke 3:21, 22.

What prophecy did Jesus quote shortly after this as applying to Himself?

"The Spirit of the Lord is upon me, because he hath anointed me to preach the gospel to the poor." Luke 4:18. (See Mark 1:15.)

NOTE—It is evident that the sixty-nine weeks (483 years) were to reach to the baptism of Christ, as that was the time of His anointing by the Holy Spirit. John the Baptist began his work in the fifteenth year of the reign of Tiberius (Luke 3:1-3), and this would put the anointing of Jesus in A.D. 27, at the time of His baptism.

When was the decree made to restore and build Jerusalem?

"This Ezra went up from Babylon. . . . And there went up some of the children of Israel, and of the priests, and the Levites, and the singers, and the porters, and the Nethinims, unto Jerusalem in the seventh year of Artaxerxes the king. And he came to Jerusalem in the seventh year of Artaxerxes the king. And he came to Jerusalem in the fifth month, which was in the seventh year of the king." Ezra 7:6-8.

NOTE—Three decrees were issued by Persian monarchs for the restoration of the Jews to their homeland. They are mentioned in the book of Ezra: "They builded, and finished it, according to the commandment of the God of Israel, and according to the commandment of Cyrus, and Darius, and Artaxerxes king of Persia." Ezra 6:14.

The decree of Cyrus pertained to the Temple only; the decree of Darius Hystaspes provided for the continuance of

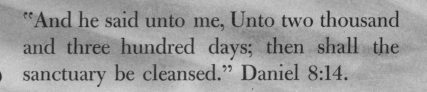

"And he said unto me, Unto two thousand and three hundred days; then shall the sanctuary be cleansed." Daniel 8:14.

7 WEEKS

62 WEEKS

ONE

457 BC

408 BC

27 AD

AD 31

DECREE

49 YEARS

434 YEARS

RESTORATION COMPLETED

MESSIAH ANOINTED

MESSIAH CUT OFF

7 YEARS

GOS

This pictorial chart delineates the longest time prophecy in the Bible. Since in Bible prophecy a day represents a literal year (Numbers 14:34, Ezekiel 4:6), the 2300-day prophecy of Daniel 8:14 points out twenty-three centuries of history from Artaxerxes' commandment to restore and rebuild Jerusalem down to A.D. 1844 when the investigative judgment began in the heavenly sanctuary.

that work, hindered by Smerdis; but the decree of Artaxerxes restored the full Jewish government, making provision for the enforcement of their laws. This last decree, therefore, is the one from which we reckon the seventy weeks, as well as the 2300 days.

The letter of Artaxerxes to Ezra, conferring upon him authority to do this work, is found in Ezra 7:11-26.

The decree of Artaxerxes was issued in the seventh year of his reign, and according to ancient methods of chronology, went into effect in Jerusalem in the fall of 457 B.C. Reckoning 483 full years from the first day of 457 B.C. would bring us to the last day of A.D. 26. This is demonstrated from the fact that it requires all of the twenty-six years A.D. and all of the 457 years B.C. to make 483 years, which may be illustrated by the diagram on pages 68, 69.

The diagram also reveals that if the decree for the complete restoration of Jerusalem did not go into effect until after Ezra reached Jerusalem, that is, until past the middle of the year 457 B.C. (Ezra 7:8), then all the time of the first part of that year not included in the period must be added to the last day of A.D. 26, which would bring us to the latter part of A.D. 27, the time of Christ's baptism. This "seals up," or makes sure, the prophecy.

At the close of 483 years, in A.D. 27, one week, or seven years of the 490, yet remained. What was to be done in the midst of that week?

"He shall confirm the covenant with many for one week: and in the midst of the week he shall cause the sacrifice and the oblation to cease." Daniel 9:27.

NOTE—As the sixty-nine weeks ended in the fall of A.D. 27, the middle of the seventieth week, or the three and a half years, would end in the spring of A.D. 31, when Christ was crucified, and by His death caused to cease, or brought to an end, the sacrifices and oblations of the earthly sanctuary. Three and a half years more (the last part of the seventieth week) would end in the autumn of A.D. 34. This brings us to the end of the 490 years which were "cut off" from the 2300. There still remain 1810 years, which, if added to A.D. 34, take us to A.D. 1844.

A.D. 1844 AND THE INVESTIGATIVE JUDGMENT

And what did the angel say would then take place?

"He said unto me, Unto two thousand and three hundred days; then shall the sanctuary be cleansed." Daniel 8:14.

NOTE—In other words, the great closing work of Christ for the world, the atonement, or the investigative judgment, would at that time begin. The typical Day of Atonement for Israel occupied but one day in a year. This may occupy but a correspondingly short time. Already that work has been going on for more than a century, and must soon close. Who is ready to meet its decisions?

Under what symbol is the importance of the judgment-hour message emphasized?

"I saw another *angel fly in the midst of heaven,* having the everlasting gospel to preach unto them that dwell on the earth, and to every nation, and kindred, and tongue, and people, *saying with a loud voice,* Fear God, and give glory to him; for the hour of his judgment is come." Revelation 14:6, 7.

NOTE—The symbol of an angel is here used to represent the message of the judgment which is to be preached to every nation. Since angels preach their messages to men through human agencies, it would be understood that this symbol of an angel flying in mid-heaven represents a great religious movement giving to men the judgment-hour message.

In view of the investigative judgment, what are we admonished to do?

"*Fear God, and give glory to him;* for the hour of his judgment is come: and *worship him that made heaven and earth, and the sea, and the fountains of waters.*" Verse 7.

What earnest admonition is given by the apostle Paul?

"The times of this ignorance God winked at; but now *commandeth all men every where to repent:* because he hath appointed a day, in the which he will judge the world in righteousness by that man whom he hath ordained; whereof he hath given assurance unto all men, in that he hath raised him from the dead." Acts 17:30, 31.

THE SANCTUARY AND TWO APARTMENTS

What did God command Israel to make?

"And let them make me a *sanctuary;* that I may dwell among them." Exodus 25:8.

What was offered in this sanctuary?

"In which were offered both gifts and sacrifices." Hebrews 9:9.

Besides the court, how many parts had this sanctuary?

"And the vail shall divide unto you between the *holy place* and the *most holy.*" Exodus 26:33.

What was in the first apartment, or holy place?

"For there was a tabernacle made; the first, wherein was the *candlestick,* and the *table,* and the *shewbread;* which is called the sanctuary." Hebrews 9:2. "And he put the golden altar in the tent of the congregation before the vail." Exodus 40:26. (See also Exodus 30:1-6.)

What was contained in the second apartment?

"And after the second veil, the tabernacle which is called the Holiest of all; which had the *golden censer, and the ark of the covenant* overlaid round about with gold, wherein was . . . the tables of the covenant." Hebrews 9:3, 4. (See also Exodus 40:20, 21.)

By what name was the cover of the ark known?

"And thou shalt put *the mercy seat* above upon the ark; and in the ark thou shalt put the testimony that I shall give thee." Exodus 25:21.

Where was God to meet with Israel?

"And there I will meet with thee, and I will commune with thee *from above the mercy seat, from between the two cherubims which are upon the ark of the testimony.*" Verse 22.

What was in the ark, under the mercy seat?

"And he wrote in the tables, according to the first writing, *the ten commandments. . . .* And I turned myself and came down from the mount, and *put the tables in the ark* which I had made." Deuteronomy 10:4, 5.

When did the priest minister in the first apartment?

"Now these things having been thus prepared, the priests go in *continually* into the first tabernacle, accomplishing the services." Hebrews 9:6, RV.

Who went into the second apartment? When and why?

"But into the second went *the high priest alone once every year, not without blood, which he offered for himself, and for the errors of the people.*" Verse 7.

THE DAILY SERVICE

What were sinners desiring pardon instructed to do?

"And if any one of the common people sin through ignorance, while he doeth somewhat against any of the commandments of the Lord . . . then he shall bring his offering, a kid of the goats, a female without blemish, for his sin which he hath sinned. *And he shall lay his hand upon the head of the sin offering, and slay the sin offering in the place of the burnt offering.*" Leviticus 4:27-29.

NOTE—According to this, if a man sinned in Israel, he violated one of the Ten Commandments that were in the ark under the mercy seat. These commandments are the foundation of God's government. To violate them is to commit sin, and so become subject to death. (1 John 3:4; Romans 6:23.) But there was a mercy seat reared above these holy and just commandments. In the dispensation of His mercy God grants the sinner the privilege of confessing his sins and bringing a substitute to meet the demands of the law, and thus of obtaining mercy.

What was done with the blood of the offering?

"And the priest shall take of the blood thereof with his finger, and put it upon the horns of the altar of burnt offering, and *shall pour out all the blood thereof at the bottom of the altar.*" Verse 30.

NOTE—After a person discovered his sin by the law which demanded the death of the transgressor, he first brought his offering; then he confessed his sin while laying his hands on the head of the victim, thus, in figure, transferring his sin to the victim; the victim was next slain in the court, or outer part of the sanctuary, and its blood put on the horns of the altar and poured at the foot of the altar. In this way sins were pardoned, and, in the typical service, transferred to the sanctuary.

THE DAY OF ATONEMENT

After this accumulation of the sins of the year, what service took place yearly on the tenth day of the seventh month?

"And this shall be a statute for ever unto you: that in the seventh month, on the tenth day of the month, ye shall afflict your souls, . . . for *on that day shall the priest make an atonement for you, to cleanse you, that ye may be clean from all your sins before the Lord.*" Leviticus 16:29, 30.

How was the sanctuary itself to be cleansed, and how were the sins of the people to be finally disposed of?

"And he [the high priest] shall take of the congregation of the children of Israel two kids of the goats for a sin offering. . . . And he shall take the two goats, and present them before the Lord at the door of the tabernacle of the congregation. And Aaron shall cast lots upon the two goats, one lot *for the Lord,* and the other lot *for the scapegoat.*" Verses 5-8.

NOTE—The Hebrew word for scapegoat is *Azazel.* See margin of verse 8. It is used as a proper name, and, according to the opinion of the most ancient Hebrews and Christians, refers to Satan, or the angel who revolted and persisted in rebellion and sin.

What was done with the blood of the goat upon which the Lord's lot fell?

"Then shall he kill the goat of the sin offering, that is for the people, and bring his blood within the vail, . . . *and sprinkle it upon the mercy seat,* and before the mercy seat." Verse 15.

Why was it necessary to make this atonement?

"And he shall make an atonement for the holy place, *because of the uncleanness of the children of Israel, and because of their transgressions in all their sins:* and so shall he do for the tabernacle of the congregation, that remaineth among them in the midst of their uncleanness." Verse 16.

NOTE—Sins were transferred to the sanctuary during the year by the blood and flesh of the sin offerings made daily at the door of the tabernacle. Here they remained until the Day of Atonement, when the high priest went into the most holy place with the blood of the goat on which the Lord's lot fell; and, bearing the accumulated sins of the year in before the mercy seat, he there, in type, atoned for them, and so cleansed the sanctuary.

After having made atonement for the people in the most holy place, what did the high priest next do?

"And when he hath made an end of reconciling the holy place, and the tabernacle of the congregation, and the altar, he shall bring the live goat: and Aaron shall lay both his hands upon the head of the live goat, and confess over him all the iniquities of the children of Israel, and all their transgressions in all their sins, putting them upon the head of the goat, and shall send him away by the hand of a fit man into the wilderness. And the goat shall bear upon him all their iniquities unto a land not inhabited: and he shall let go the goat in the wilderness." Verses 20-22.

NOTE—The offering of the Lord's goat cleansed the sanctuary. By this offering the sins of the people, transferred there during the year, were, in type, atoned for; but they were not by this offering finally disposed of, or destroyed. The scapegoat, symbolizing Satan, the great tempter and originator of sin, was brought to the sanctuary, and upon his head were placed these already atoned-for sins. The sending away of the goat into the wilderness separated the sins forever from the people. (On the scapegoat see M'Clintock and Strong, *Cyclopaedia of Biblical, Theological, and Ecclesiastical Literature,* vol. 9, pp. 397, 398, art. "Scapegoat"; *The Encyclopedic Dictionary,* vol. 1, p. 397; *The New Schaff-Herzog Encyclopedia of Religious Knowledge,* vol. 1, p. 389, art. "Azazel.")

A TYPE OF THE HEAVENLY SANCTUARY

What was this earthly sanctuary and its round of service?

"Which was a *figure* for the time then present." Hebrews 9:9.

Of what sanctuary, or tabernacle, is Christ the minister?

"A minister of the sanctuary, and of the true tabernacle, *which the Lord pitched, and not man."* Hebrews 8:2.

Of what was the blood of all the sacrifices of the former dispensation only a type?

"Neither by the blood of goats and calves, but *by his own blood* he entered in once into the holy place, having obtained eternal redemption for us." Hebrews 9:12. (See Ephesians 5:2.)

NOTE—Through the sacrifices and offerings brought to the altar of the earthly sanctuary, the penitent believer was to lay hold of the merits of Christ, the Saviour to come. In this way, and in this way only, was there any virtue connected with them.

At Christ's death, what miracle signified that the priestly services of the earthly sanctuary were finished?

"Jesus, when he had cried again with a loud voice, yielded up the ghost. And, behold, *the veil of the temple was rent in twain from the top to the bottom."* Matthew 27:50, 51.

NOTE—Type had met antitype; the shadow had reached the substance. Christ, the great Sacrifice, had been slain, and was now to enter upon His work as our great High Priest in the sanctuary in heaven. The priestly work in the earthly sanctuary was typical of the work of Christ in the heavenly sanctuary.

How are the heavenly and earthly sanctuaries related?

"Who serve unto the *example* and *shadow* of heavenly things, as Moses was admonished of God when he was about to make the tabernacle: for, See, saith he, that thou make all things according to the *pattern* shewed to thee in the mount." Hebrews 8:5.

By what comparison is it shown that the heavenly sanctuary will be cleansed?

"It was therefore necessary that the patterns of things in the heavens should be purified with these; *but the heavenly things themselves with better sacrifices than these."* Hebrews 9:23.

When Christ has finished His priestly mediatorial

work in the heavenly sanctuary, what decree will go forth?

"He that is unjust, let him be unjust still: and he which is filthy, let him be filthy still: and he that is righteous, let him be righteous still: and he that is holy, let him be holy still." Revelation 22:11.

NOTE—This declaration is made immediately before the coming of Christ in the clouds of heaven.

According to Daniel's vision of the judgment, what is to be given to Christ while He is still before the Father?

"I saw . . . , and, behold, one like the Son of man came . . . to the Ancient of days, and they brought him near before him. And there was given him *dominion*, and *glory*, and *a kingdom*, that all people, nations, and languages, should serve him." Daniel 7:13, 14.

What will occur when the Lord descends from heaven?

"For the Lord himself shall descend from heaven with a shout, with the voice of the archangel, and with the trump of God: and *the dead in Christ shall rise first: then we which are alive and remain shall be caught up together with them in the clouds, to meet the Lord in the air:* and so shall we ever be with the Lord." 1 Thessalonians 4:16, 17.

What statement immediately following the announcement mentioned in Revelation 22:11 indicates that a judgment work has been in progress before Christ comes?

"And, behold, I come quickly; and *my reward is with me, to give every man according as his work shall be.*" Revelation 22:12.

NOTE—The typical sanctuary service is fully met in the work of Christ. As the atonement day of the former dispensation was really a day of judgment, so the atonement work of Christ will include the investigation of the cases of his people prior to his coming the second time to receive them unto Himself.

NATURE AND TIME OF THE MESSAGE

What prophetic view of the judgment was given Daniel?

"I beheld till the thrones were cast down [literally, "placed"], and the Ancient of days did sit. . . . Thousand thousands ministered unto him, and ten thousand times ten thousand stood before him: the judgment was set, and the books were opened." Daniel 7:9, 10.

What assurance has God given of the judgment?

"Because *he hath appointed a day, in the which he will judge the world* in righteousness by that man whom he hath ordained; whereof he hath given

assurance unto all men, *in that he hath raised him from the dead."* Acts 17:31.

What message announces the judgment hour is come?

"And I saw another angel fly in the midst of heaven, having the everlasting gospel to preach unto them that dwell on the earth, and to every nation, and kindred, and tongue, and people, saying with a loud voice, Fear God, and give glory to him; for *the hour of his judgment is come:* and worship him that made heaven, and earth, and the sea, and the fountains of waters." Revelation 14:6, 7.

In view of the judgment hour, what is proclaimed anew?

"The everlasting gospel." Verse 6.

How extensively is this message to be proclaimed?

"To *every nation,* and *kindred,* and *tongue,* and *people."* Verse 6.

What is the whole world called upon to do?

"Fear God, and give glory to him." Verse 7.

What special reason is given for this?

"For *the hour of his judgment is come."* Verse 7.

Whom are all called upon to worship?

"Him that made heaven, and earth." Verse 7.

NOTE—There is only one gospel (Romans 1:16, 17; Galatians 1:8), first announced in Eden (Genesis 3:15), preached to Abraham (Galatians 3:8) and to the children of Israel (Hebrews 4:1, 2), and proclaimed anew in every generation. In its development the gospel meets the needs of every crisis in the world's history. John the Baptist in his preaching announced the kingdom of heaven at hand (Matthew 3:1, 2), and prepared the way for the first advent. (John 1:22, 23.) Christ Himself, in His preaching of the gospel, announced the fulfillment of a definite-time prophecy (the sixty-nine weeks, or 483 years, of Daniel 9:25), and called the people to repentance, in view of the coming of the predicted Messiah. (Mark 1:14, 15.) So when the time for the judgment comes, and Christ's second advent is near, a worldwide announcement of these events is to be made in the preaching of the everlasting gospel adapted to meet the need of the hour.

What prophetic period extends to the time of the cleansing of the sanctuary, or the investigative judgment?

"And he said unto me, Unto *two thousand and three hundred days;* then shall the sanctuary be cleansed." Daniel 8:14.

When did this long period expire?

In A.D. 1844. See pages 68 and 69.

NOTE—The whole period extends to the time of the judgment, just preceding the Second Advent, and at its expiration a special gospel message is sent to all the world, proclaiming the judgment hour at hand and calling upon all to worship the Creator. The facts of history answer to this interpretation of the prophecy, for at this very time (1844) just such a message was being proclaimed in various parts of the world. This was the beginning of the great Second Advent message which is now being proclaimed throughout the world.

CALL TO WORSHIP THE CREATOR

How is the true God distinguished from all false gods?

"Thus shall ye say unto them, *The gods that have not made the heavens and the earth,* even they shall perish from the earth. . . . *He [the true God] hath made the earth by his power, he hath established the world by his wisdom, and hath stretched out the heavens by his discretion."* Jeremiah 10:11, 12.

For what reason is worship justly due to God?

"For the Lord is a great God, and a great King above all gods. . . . *The sea is his, and he made it: and his hands formed the dry land.* O come, let us worship and bow down: let us kneel before the Lord our *maker."* Psalm 95:3-6.

Why do the inhabitants of heaven worship God?

"The four and twenty elders fall down before him, . . . saying, Thou art worthy, O Lord, to receive glory and honour and power: *for thou hast created all things,* and for thy pleasure they are and were created." Revelation 4:10, 11.

What memorial of His creative power did God establish?

"Remember *the sabbath day,* to keep it holy. . . . *For in six days the Lord made heaven and earth, the sea, and all that in them is,* and rested the seventh day: wherefore the Lord blessed the sabbath day, and hallowed it." Exodus 20:8-11.

What place has the Sabbath in the work of salvation?

"Moreover also I gave them my sabbaths, to be *a sign* between me and them, that they might know that I am the Lord that *sanctify* them." Ezekiel 20:12.

THE STANDARD FOR ALL

How many are concerned in the judgment?

"For we must *all* appear before the judgment seat of Christ; that *every one* may receive the things done in his body, *according to that he hath done, whether it be good or bad."* 2 Corinthians 5:10.

What will be the standard in the judgment?

"For whosoever shall keep the whole law, and yet offend in one point, he is guilty of all. For he that said, Do not commit adultery, said also, Do not kill. Now if thou commit no adultery, yet if thou kill, thou art become a transgressor of the law. So speak ye, and so do, as they that shall be judged *by the law of liberty."* James 2:10-12.

In view of the judgment, what exhortation is given?

"Let us hear the conclusion of the whole matter: *Fear God, and keep his commandments:* for this is the whole duty of man. For God shall bring every work into judgment, with every secret thing, whether it be good, or whether it be evil." Ecclesiastes 12:13, 14.

NOTE—A comparison of Revelation 14:7 with Ecclesiastes 12:13 suggests that the way to give glory to God is to keep His commandments, and that in giving the judgment-hour message, the duty of keeping the commandments would be emphasized. This is plainly shown in the description given of the people who are gathered out of every nation, kindred, tongue, and people as the result of the preaching of this message, in connection with other messages which immediately follow and accompany it. Of this people it is said, "Here are they that keep the commandments of God, and the faith of Jesus." Revelation 14:12.

Good News About
GROWTH IN CHRIST

GRACE MULTIPLIED

How does the apostle Peter close his second epistle?

"But *grow in grace,* and in the knowledge of our Lord and Saviour Jesus Christ." 2 Peter 3:18.

How may grace and peace be multiplied in believers?

"Grace and peace be multiplied unto you *through the knowledge of God, and of Jesus our Lord."* 2 Peter 1:2.

What is implied in a knowledge of God and Jesus Christ?

"And *this is life eternal,* that they might know thee the only true God, and Jesus Christ, whom thou hast sent." John 17:3.

By what may we be partakers of the divine nature?

"Whereby are given unto us *exceeding great and precious promises:* that by these ye might be partakers of the divine nature, having escaped the corruption that is in the world through lust." 2 Peter 1:4.

GRACE BY ADDITION

What graces are we to add in our character building?

"Add to your faith *virtue;* and to virtue *knowledge;* and to knowledge *temperance* [self-control]; and to temperance *patience;* and to patience *godliness;* and to godliness *brotherly kindness;* and to brotherly kindness *charity."* Verses 5-7.

NOTE—*Faith* is the first round in the Christian ladder, the first step Godward. "He that cometh to God must *believe."* Hebrews 11:6.

But an inoperative faith is useless. "Faith without *works* is dead." James 2:20. To be of value, there must be coupled with faith *virtue,* or *moral excellence.*

To moral excellence there needs to be added *knowledge;* otherwise, like the stumbling Jews, one may have a zeal, "but *not according to knowledge."* Romans 10:2. Fanaticism is the result of such courage, or zeal. Knowledge, therefore, is an essential to healthy Christian growth.

To knowledge there needs to be added *temperance,* or *self-control—self-government.* To know to do good, and not do it, is as useless as is faith without works. (See James 4:17.)

Patience, or *steadfast endurance,* naturally follows *temperance,* or *self-control.* It is well-nigh impossible for an intemperate person to be *patient.*

Having gained control of oneself, and become patient, one is in a condition to manifest *godliness,* or *Godlikeness.*

Kindness toward the brethren, or *brotherly kindness,* naturally follows godliness.

Charity, or love for *all,* even our *enemies,* is the crowning grace, the highest step, the eighth round, in the Christian ladder.

The arrangement in this enumeration of graces is by no means accidental or haphazard, but logical and sequential, each following the other in natural, necessary order. The finger of Inspiration is seen here.

What is said of charity in the Scriptures?

"Charity *suffereth long, and is kind; . . . thinketh no evil; rejoiceth not in iniquity, but rejoiceth in the truth; beareth all things, believeth all things, hopeth all things, endureth all things."* 1 Corinthians 13:4-7. "And above all things have fervent charity among yourselves: for charity *shall cover the multitude of sins."* 1 Peter 4:8.

NOTE—*Charity* and *love* are translations of the same Greek word. Instead of *charity* most versions read *love.*

What is charity called?

"And above all these things put on charity, which is *the bond of perfectness."* Colossians 3:14.

What is the result of cultivating these eight graces?

"For if these things be in you, and abound, *they make you that ye shall neither be barren nor unfruitful in the knowledge of our Lord Jesus Christ."* 2 Peter 1:8.

What is the condition of one who lacks these graces?

"But he that lacketh these things *is blind, and cannot see afar off, and hath forgotten that he was purged from his old sins."* Verse 9.

What is promised those who add grace to grace?

"If ye do these things, *ye shall never fall."* Verse 10.

What power was to make war upon the remnant church prior to the second advent of the Saviour to this earth?

"And *the dragon* [Satan] was wroth with the woman, and went to make war with the remnant of her seed, which keep the commandments of God, and have the testimony of Jesus Christ." Revelation 12:17.

What reward is promised to all who overcome each besetting sin?

"To him that overcometh will I *give to eat of the tree of life,* which is in the midst of the paradise of God." Revelation 2:7. (See also Revelation 2:11, 17, 26-28; 3:5, 12, 21.) "He that overcometh shall inherit *all things.*" Revelation 21:7.

THE CONQUERING LEADER

Through whom are we able to conquer the power that wars against us?

"Nay, in all these things we are more than conquerors *through him that loved us.*" Romans 8:37.

Who was the invisible leader of the armies of Israel?

"Behold, there stood a man over against him with his sword drawn in his hand: and Joshua went unto him, and said unto him, Art thou for us, or for our adversaries? And he said, Nay; but as *captain of the host of the Lord* am I now come." Joshua 5:13, 14. (See also 1 Corinthians 10:1-4.)

WEAPONS FOR WARFARE

What is the character of the Christian's weapons of warfare?

"For the weapons of our warfare are *not carnal, but mighty through God to the pulling down of strong holds.*" 2 Corinthians 10:4.

What are these weapons able to conquer?

"Casting down *imaginations,* and *every high thing that exalteth itself against the knowledge of God,* and bringing into captivity *every thought* to the obedience of Christ." Verse 5.

What are we to put on?

"Put on the whole armour of God, that ye may be able to stand against the wiles of the devil." Ephesians 6:11.

With what kind of forces do we have to contend?

"For we wrestle not against flesh and blood, but against *principalities,* against *powers,* against *the rulers of the darkness of this world,* against *spiritual wickedness in high places.*" Verse 12.

> NOTE—"Spiritual wickedness in high places" is more accurately rendered, "wicked spirits in heavenly places."

What are the first essentials of the needed armor?

"Stand therefore, having your *loins girt about with truth,* and having on the *breastplate of righteousness.*" Verse 14.

With what are the feet of the children of God to be shod?

"And your feet shod with *the preparation of the gospel of peace.*" Verse 15. (See also Ephesians 2:14; James 3:18.)

What piece of armor is next mentioned as necessary?

"Above all, taking *the shield of faith,* wherewith ye shall be able to quench all the fiery darts of the wicked." Ephesians 6:16. (See 1 John 5:4; Hebrews 11:6.)

What armor is to be put on as a protection to the head?

"And take *the helmet of salvation.*" Ephesians 6:17.

> NOTE—In 1 Thessalonians 5:8 the helmet is called "the *hope* of salvation." The helmet was worn to protect the head. So the hope of salvation will preserve the courage, and thus aid in protecting the spiritual life of the Christian pilgrim when beset by the enemy of righteousness.

What is the sword of the Christian soldier?

"The sword of the Spirit, which is *the word of God."* Ephesians 6:17.

> NOTE—By this Christ defeated the enemy. (See Matthew 4:1-11; Luke 4:1-13.) But no one can *use this sword* who does not *know* it. Hence, the importance of studying and knowing for oneself what the Bible teaches.

FAITHFULNESS AND VICTORY

In what words are the courage, faithfulness, and loyalty of the church expressed?

"And they overcame him by the blood of the Lamb, and by the word of their testimony; and *they loved not their lives unto the death.*" Revelation 12:11.

Will Christ's loyal soldiers be victorious under Him?

"And I saw as it were a sea of glass mingled with fire: and them that had *gotten the victory* over the beast, and over his image, and over his mark, and over the number of his name, stand on the sea of glass, having the harps of God." Revelation 15:2.

GOD'S PROMISES REGARDING PRAYER

By what title does the psalmist address God?

"O thou that hearest prayer, unto thee shall all flesh come." Psalm 65:2.

Of whom does the Bible teach that God is a rewarder?

"A rewarder *of them that diligently seek him.*" Hebrews 11:6.

Christ Our High Priest
Harry Anderson, Artist

How willing is God to hear and answer prayer?

"If ye then, being evil, know how to give good gifts unto your children, *how much more shall your Father which is in heaven give good things to them that ask him?*" Matthew 7:11.

What above all else shows God's willingness to do this?

"He that spared not his own Son, but delivered him up for us all, how shall he not with him also freely give us all things?" Romans 8:32.

THE FIRST STEP IN PRAYER

Upon what conditions are we promised needed blessings?

"*Ask,* and it shall be given you; *seek,* and ye shall find; *knock,* and it shall be opened unto you: for every one that asketh receiveth; and he that seeketh findeth; and to him that knocketh it shall be opened." Matthew 7:7, 8.

NOTE—"Prayer is the opening of the heart to God as to a friend."—E. G. WHITE, *Steps to Christ* (pocket ed.), p. 93. Prayer does not change God; but it does change *us* and *our relation* to God. It places us in the channel of blessings, and in that frame of mind in which God can consistently and safely grant our requests.

"How shall we pray so as to be heard and to receive help? For one thing, there must be a real desire in our hearts. Forms of words do not make prayer: we must want something, and must realize our dependence upon God for it."—J. R. MILLER.

From whom do all good and perfect gifts come?

"Every good gift and every perfect gift is from above, and cometh down from *the Father of lights,* with whom is no variableness, neither shadow of turning." James 1:17.

If one lacks wisdom, what is he told to do?

"If any of you lack wisdom, *let him ask of God,* that giveth to all men liberally, and upbraideth not; and it shall be given him." Verse 5.

THREE CONDITIONS TO ANSWERED PRAYER

How must one ask in order to receive?

"But let him *ask in faith, nothing wavering.* For he that wavereth is like a wave of the sea driven with the wind and tossed. For let not that man think that he shall receive any thing of the Lord." Verses 6, 7. (See Mark 11:24.)

Under what condition does the Lord not hear prayer?

"*If I regard iniquity in my heart,* the Lord will not hear me." Psalm 66:18. (See Isaiah 59:1, 2; James 4:3.)

Whose prayers does Solomon say are an abomination?

"*He that turneth away his ear from hearing the law, even his prayer shall be abomination.*" Proverbs 28:9.

NOTE—Contention and discord quench the spirit of prayer. (1 Peter 3:1-7.) Many grieve the Spirit and drive Christ from their homes by giving way to impatience and passion. Angels of God flee from homes where there are unkind words, contention, and strife.

For whom did Christ teach us to pray?

"But I say unto you, Love your enemies, bless them that curse you, do good to them that hate you, and *pray for them which despitefully use you, and persecute you.*" Matthew 5:44.

NOTE—We cannot hate those for whom we pray sincerely.

When praying, what must we do in order to be forgiven?

"And when ye stand praying, *forgive, if ye have ought against any:* that your Father also which is in heaven may forgive you your trespasses." Mark 11:25.

TIME, PLACE, AND CONTENT OF PRAYER

What did Christ say concerning secret prayer?

"But thou, when thou prayest, *enter into thy closet,* and when thou hast shut thy door, *pray to thy Father which is in secret;* and thy Father which seeth in secret shall reward thee openly." Matthew 6:6.

To what place did Jesus retire for secret devotion?

"And when he had sent the multitudes away, *he went up into a mountain apart to pray:* and when the evening was come, he was there alone." Matthew 14:23.

With what should our prayers be mingled?

"Be careful for nothing; but in every thing by prayer and supplication *with thanksgiving* let your requests be made known unto God." Philippians 4:6.

How often should we pray?

"*Praying always* with all prayer and supplication in the Spirit." Ephesians 6:18. "*Pray without ceasing.*" 1 Thessalonians 5:17. "*Every day will I bless thee;* and I will praise thy name for ever and ever." Psalm 145:2.

How often did the psalmist say he would pray?

"*Evening,* and *morning,* and at *noon,* will I pray, and cry aloud: and he shall hear my voice." Psalm 55:17. (See Daniel 6:10.)

In whose name did Christ teach us to pray?

"And whatsoever ye shall ask in *my name,* that will I do." John 14:13.

The Power of Prayer

Mitchell Heinze, Artist
© 1989 R&H

Why did the unjust judge answer the widow's prayer?

"Though I fear not God, nor regard man; yet *because this widow troubleth me,* I will avenge her, lest *by her continual coming she weary me."* Luke 18:4, 5.

NOTE—The lesson of the parable is that "men ought always to pray, and not to faint." Verse 1. If this woman, by her persistence in asking, obtained her request from such a man, surely God, who is just, will answer the earnest, persistent prayers of His people, though the answer may be long delayed.

SUBJECTS OF MEDITATION

What was one of Paul's injunctions to Timothy?

"*Meditate upon these things;* give thyself wholly to them." 1 Timothy 4:15.

NOTE—Meditation is to the soul what digestion is to the body. It assimilates, appropriates, and makes personal and practical that which has been seen, heard, or read.

When did the psalmist say he would praise God with joyful lips?

"*When I remember thee* upon my bed, *and meditate on thee* in the night watches." Psalm 63:6.

How will such meditation be to one who loves God?

"My meditation of him shall be *sweet."* Psalm 104:34.

In what does the psalmist say the man who is blessed delight and meditate?

"His delight is in *the law of the Lord;* and in *his law* doth he meditate day and night." Psalm 1:2.

TEMPTATION AND MEDITATION

With what adversary do we constantly have to contend?

"Be sober, be vigilant; because *your adversary the devil,* as a roaring lion, walketh about, seeking whom he may devour." 1 Peter 5:8.

When is a man tempted?

"But every man is tempted, when *he is drawn away of his own lust, and enticed."* James 1:14.

That we may not be overcome, what are we told to do?

"*Watch and pray, that ye enter not into temptation:* the spirit indeed is willing, but the flesh is weak." Matthew 26:41.

NECESSITY OF CONSTANT PRAYER ATTITUDE

How constantly should we pray?

"Pray *without ceasing."* 1 Thessalonians 5:17.

"Continuing *instant in prayer."* Romans 12:12.

NOTE—This does not mean that we should be constantly bowed before God in prayer, but that we should not *neglect* prayer, and that we should *ever be in a prayerful frame of mind,* even when walking by the way or engaged in the duties of life—ever ready to send up our petitions to heaven for help in time of need.

PREPARATION FOR CHRIST'S RETURN

That we might be prepared for His coming, what admonition did Christ give?

"*Take ye heed, watch and pray:* for ye know not when the time is. . . . And what I say unto you I say unto all, *Watch."* Mark 13:33-37. (See also Luke 21:36.)

Why are watchfulness and prayer especially imperative in the last days?

"Woe to the inhabiters of the earth and of the sea! for the devil is come down unto you, having great wrath, because he knoweth that he hath but a short time." Revelation 12:12.

GOD'S UNLIMITED ABILITY

How does God anticipate the needs of His children?

"And it shall come to pass, that *before they call, I will answer;* and while they are yet speaking, I will hear." Isaiah 65:24.

Is there any limit to God's ability to help?

"Now unto him that is *able to do exceeding abundantly above all that we ask or think."* Ephesians 3:20.

How fully has God promised to supply our needs?

"My God *shall supply all your need* according to his riches in glory by Christ Jesus." Philippians 4:19.

MAN'S LIMITED UNDERSTANDING

Do we always know what to pray for?

"Likewise the Spirit also helpeth our infirmities: *for we know not what we should pray for as we ought."* Romans 8:26.

Does God always see fit to grant our petitions?

"For this thing I besought the Lord thrice, that it might depart from me. And he said unto me, My grace is sufficient for thee: for my strength is made perfect in weakness." 2 Corinthians 12:8, 9.

NOTE—Paul's affliction, some have thought, was impaired sight. (Acts 9:8, 9, 18; 22:11-13.) The retaining of such an imperfection would be a constant reminder to him of his conversion, and hence a blessing in disguise.

PATIENCE AND PERSEVERANCE

If an answer does not come at once, what should we do?
"Rest in the Lord, and *wait patiently for him.*" Psalm 37:7.

Why was the parable of the importunate widow given?
"And he spake a parable unto them to this end, *that men ought always to pray, and not to faint.*" Luke 18:1.

NOTE—The request of the importunate widow was granted because of her persistency. God wants us to *seek* Him, and to seek Him *earnestly,* when we pray. He is a rewarder of them that *diligently* seek Him. (Hebrews 11:6.)

How did Elijah pray before obtaining his request?
"Elias was a man subject to like passions as we are, and *he prayed earnestly* that it might not rain: and it rained not on the earth by the space of three years and six months. And he prayed again, and the heaven gave rain, and the earth brought forth her fruit." James 5:17, 18. (See Revelation 11:3-6.)

TWO FUNDAMENTAL CONDITIONS

Upon what condition does Christ say we shall receive?
"Therefore I say unto you, What things soever ye desire, when ye pray, *believe that ye receive them, and ye shall have them.*" Mark 11:24.

Without this faith, will God answer prayer?
"*But let him ask in faith, nothing wavering.* For he that wavereth is like a wave of the sea driven with the wind and tossed. For *let not that man think that he shall receive any thing of the Lord.*" James 1:6, 7.

What petitions may we confidently expect God to hear?
"And this is the confidence that we have in him, that, *if we ask any thing according to his will,* he heareth us: and if we know that he hear us, whatsoever we ask, we know that we have the petitions that we desired of him." 1 John 5:14, 15.

NOTE—God's will is expressed in His law, His promises, and His word. (Psalm 40:8; Romans 2:17, 18; 1 Peter 1:4.)

EXAMPLES OF ANSWERED PRAYER

When Daniel and his fellows were about to be slain because the wise men of Babylon could not reveal to Nebuchadnezzar his dream, how did God answer their united prayers?
"*Then was the secret revealed unto Daniel in a night vision.* Then Daniel blessed the God of heaven." Daniel 2:19.

NOTE—In 1839 the sultan of Turkey decreed that not a representative of the Christian religion should remain in the empire. Learning of this, Dr. William Goodell, an American missionary to Turkey, came home to his friend and colleague, Dr. Cyrus Hamlin, the first president of Robert College, Constantinople, with the sad news: "It is all over with us; we have to leave. The American consul and the British ambassador say it is no use to meet with antagonism this violent and vindictive monarch." To this Dr. Hamlin replied: "The Sultan of the universe can, in answer to prayer, change the decree of the sultan of Turkey." They gave themselves to prayer. The next day the sultan died, and the decree was never executed. (See Daniel 4:17, 24, 25.)

When Peter was imprisoned and about to be executed by Herod, what did the church do?
"Peter therefore was kept in prison: but *prayer was made without ceasing of the church unto God for him.*" Acts 12:5.

How were their prayers answered?
"Behold, the angel of the Lord came upon him, . . . and he saith unto him, Cast thy garment about thee, and follow me. . . . And they went out, and passed on through one street; and forthwith the angel departed from him." Verses 7-10.

Because Solomon asked for wisdom rather than for long life and riches, what besides wisdom did God give him?
"Because thou hast asked this thing, . . . behold, I have done according to thy words: lo, I have given thee a wise and an understanding heart. . . . And I have also given thee that which thou hast not asked, *both riches, and honour.*" 1 Kings 3:11-13.

NOTE—The following are some things we are taught in the Scriptures to pray for: (1) For daily bread. Matthew 6:11. (2) For the forgiveness of sin. 2 Chronicles 7:14; Psalm 32:5, 6; 1 John 1:9; 5:16. (3) For the Holy Spirit. Luke 11:13; Zechariah 10:1; John 14:16. (4) For deliverance in the hour of temptation and danger. Matthew 6:13; John 17:11, 15; Proverbs 3:26; Psalm 91; Matthew 24:20. (5) For wisdom and understanding. James 1:5; 1 Kings 3:9; Daniel 2:17-19. (6) For peaceable and quiet lives. 1 Timothy 2:1, 2. (7) For the healing of the sick. James 5:14, 15; 2 Kings 20:1-11. (8) For the prosperity of the ministers of God and the gospel. Ephesians 6:18, 19; Colossians 4:3; 2 Thessalonians 3:1. (9) For those who suffer for the truth's sake. Hebrews 13:3; Acts 12:5. (10) For kings, rulers, and all in authority. 1 Timothy 2:1, 2; Ezra 6:10. (11) For temporal prosperity. 2 Corinthians 9:10; James 5:17, 18. (12) For our enemies. Matthew 5:44. (13) For all saints. Ephesians 6:18. (14) For all men. 1 Timothy 2:1. (15) For the Lord to vindicate His cause. 1 Kings 18:30-39. (16) For the coming of Christ and of God's kingdom. Matthew 6:10; Revelation 22:20.

Good News About
GOD'S PEOPLE

A WOMAN CLOTHED WITH THE SUN

Under what figure was the Christian church represented to the Apostle John?

"And there appeared a great wonder [margin, "sign"] in heaven; *a woman* clothed with the sun, and the moon under her feet, and upon her head a crown of twelve stars." Revelation 12:1.

> NOTE.—Frequently in the Scriptures a woman is used to represent the church. (See Jeremiah 6:2; 2 Corinthians 11:2.) The sun represents the light of the gospel with which the church was clothed at the first advent (1 John 2:8); the moon under her feet, the waning light of the former dispensation; and the twelve stars, the twelve apostles.

How is the church at the first advent described?

"And she being with child cried, travailing in birth, and pained to be delivered." Revelation 12:2.

> NOTE.—The church is in labor and pain while she brings forth Christ and her children, in the midst of afflictions and persecutions. (See Romans 8:19, 22; 1 John 3:1, 2; 2 Timothy 3:12.)

How are the birth, work, and ascension of Christ briefly described?

"And she brought forth a man child, who was to rule all nations with a rod of iron: and her child was caught up unto God, and to his throne." Revelation 12:5.

> NOTE.—That this passage refers to Christ is clearly evident when it is compared with Psalm 2:7-9.

THE GREAT RED DRAGON

What other sign, or wonder, appeared in heaven?

"And there appeared another wonder in heaven; and behold *a great red dragon,* having seven heads and ten horns, and seven crowns upon his heads. And his tail drew the third part of the stars of heaven, and did cast them to the earth: and the dragon stood before the woman which was ready to be delivered, for to devour her child as soon as it was born." Revelation 12:3, 4.

Who is this dragon said to be?

"And the great dragon was cast out, *that old serpent,* called the *Devil,* and *Satan,* which deceiveth the whole world." Verse 9.

> NOTE.—Primarily the dragon represents Satan, the great enemy and persecutor of the church in all ages. But Satan works through principalities and powers in his efforts to destroy the people of God. It was through a Roman king, King Herod, that he sought to destroy Christ as soon as He was born. (Matthew 2:16.) Rome must therefore also be symbolized by the dragon. The seven heads of the dragon are interpreted by some to refer to the "seven hills" upon which the city of Rome is built; by others, to the seven forms of government through which Rome passed; and by still others, and more broadly, to the seven great monarchies which have oppressed the people of God, namely, Egypt, Assyria, Chaldea, Persia, Greece, pagan Rome, and papal Rome, in either of which Rome is represented and included. (See pages 87 and 88.) The ten horns, as in the fourth beast of Daniel 7, evidently refer to the kingdoms into which Rome was finally divided, and thus again identify the dragon with the Roman power.

How is the conflict in heaven described?

"And there was war in heaven: Michael and his angels fought against the dragon; and the dragon fought and his angels, and prevailed not; neither was their place found any more in heaven. And the great dragon was cast out, that old serpent, called the Devil, and Satan, which deceiveth the whole world: he was cast out into the earth, and his angels were cast out with him." Revelation 12:7-9.

> NOTE.—This conflict, begun in heaven, continues on earth. Near the close of Christ's ministry He said, "I beheld Satan as lightning *fall from heaven.*" Luke 10:18. "Now is the judgment of this world: now shall the prince of this world be *cast out.*" John 12:31. From the councils of the representatives of the various worlds to which Satan, as the prince of this world, was formerly admitted (Job 1:6, 7; 2:1, 2), he was cast out when he crucified Christ.

What shout of triumph was heard in heaven following the victory gained by Christ?

"And I heard a loud voice saying in heaven, *Now is come salvation, and strength, and the kingdom of our God, and the power of his Christ:* for the accuser of our brethren is *cast down,* which accused them before our God day and night." Revelation 12:10-12.

PERSECUTION ON EARTH

Why was woe at this time proclaimed to the world?

"Woe to the inhabiters of the earth and of the sea! *for the devil is come down unto you, having great wrath, because he knoweth that he hath but a short time.*" Verse 12.

NOTE.—This shows that, since the crucifixion of Christ, Satan knows that his doom is sealed and that he has but a limited time in which to work, also that his efforts are now largely if not wholly confined to this world and concentrated upon its inhabitants.

What did the dragon do when cast to the earth?

"And when the dragon saw that he was cast unto the earth, *he persecuted the woman* which brought forth the man child." Verse 13.

NOTE.—The persecution of Christians began under pagan Rome, but was carried on far more extensively under papal Rome. (Matthew 24:21, 22.)

What period of time was allotted to this great persecution of God's people under papal Rome?

"And to the woman were given two wings of a great eagle, that she might fly into the wilderness, into her place, where she is nourished for *a time, and times, and half a time,* from the face of the serpent." Revelation 12:14.

NOTE.—This is the same period as that of Daniel 7:25, and, like the ten horns, identifies the dragon with the fourth beast of Daniel 7, and its later work with the work of the little horn of that same beast. In Revelation 13:5 this period is referred to as "forty and two months," and in Revelation 12:6 as 1260 days, each representing 1260 literal years, the period allotted to the supremacy of papal Rome. Beginning in A.D. 538, it ended in 1798, when the pope was taken prisoner by the French. The woman fleeing into the wilderness fittingly describes the condition of the church during those times of bitter persecution.

What was Satan's plan in persecuting the church?

"And the serpent cast out of his mouth water as a flood after the woman, *that he might cause her to be carried away of the flood.*" Verse 15.

How was the flood stayed, and Satan defeated?

"*And the earth helped the woman,* and the earth opened her mouth, and swallowed up the flood which the dragon cast out of his mouth." Verse 16.

NOTE.—The mountain fastnesses, quiet retreats, and secluded valleys of Europe for centuries shielded many who refused allegiance to the Papacy. Here, too, may be seen the results of the work of the Reformation of the sixteenth century, when some of the governments of Europe came to the help of various reform groups by staying the hand of persecution and protecting the lives of those who dared to take their stand against the Papacy. The discovery of America and the opening up of this country as an asylum for the oppressed of Europe at this time may also be included in the "help" here referred to.

What did Christ say would be the result if the days of persecution were not shortened?

"Except those days should be shortened, *there should no flesh be saved:* but for the elect's sake those days shall be shortened." Matthew 24:22.

How does Satan manifest his enmity against the remnant church?

"And the dragon was wroth with the woman, and *went to make war with the remnant of her seed,* which keep the commandments of God, and have the testimony of Jesus Christ." Revelation 12:17.

A WARNING AGAINST FALSE WORSHIP

What indicates that the messages of the judgment hour and the fall of Babylon are two parts of a threefold message?

"And *the third angel followed them.*" Revelation 14:9.

What apostasy from the worship of God is named here?

"If any man *worship the beast and his image, and receive his mark* in his forehead, or in his hand." Verse 9.

What is to be the fate of those who, instead of worshiping God, engage in this false worship?

"*The same shall drink of the wine of the wrath of God, which is poured out without mixture into the cup of his indignation;* and he shall be tormented with fire and brimstone in the presence of the holy angels, and in the presence of the Lamb: and the smoke of their torment ascendeth up for ever and ever: and they have no rest day nor night, who worship the beast and his image, and whosoever receiveth the mark of his name." Verses 10, 11. (See Isaiah 33:13; 34:1-10; Hebrews 12:29.)

How are those described who heed this warning?

"Here is the patience of the saints: here are they that keep the commandments of God, and the faith of Jesus." Revelation 14:12.

WHO IS THE BEAST POWER?

What description is given of the beast against whose worship this closing warning message is given?

"And I stood upon the sand of the sea, and saw a beast rise up out of the sea, having seven heads and ten horns, and upon his horns ten crowns, and upon his heads the name of blasphemy. And the beast which I saw was like unto a leopard, and his feet were as the feet of a bear, and his mouth as the mouth of a lion: and the dragon gave him his power, and his seat, and great authority." Revelation 13:1, 2.

NOTE.—In this composite beast from the sea are combined the symbols of the seventh chapter of Daniel, representing the Roman, Greco-Macedonian, Medio-Persian, and Babylonian empires. Its blasphemous words, its persecution of the saints, and its allotted time (verses 5-7) show that this beast, under one of its seven-headed manifestations, is identical with the little horn of the vision of Daniel 7, modern Babylon, the Papacy. The worship of the beast is the rendering of that homage to the Papacy which is due to God alone. The system of religion enforced by the Papacy contains the paganism of Babylon, Persia, Greece, and Rome, indicated by the beast's composite character (verse 2), disguised under the forms and names of Christianity. The Roman Pontifex Maximus, for instance, was continued in the pope, who is the head of the Roman priesthood. But this scripture in Revelation shows that the pope's power and his seat and his great authority do not come from Christ.

What challenge is made by those who worship the beast?

"And they worshipped the dragon which gave power unto the beast: and they worshipped the beast, saying, *Who is like unto the beast? who is able to make war with him?*" Verse 4.

Whose sovereignty is thus challenged?

"Forasmuch as *there is none like unto thee, O Lord;* thou art great, and thy name is great in might." Jeremiah 10:6. (See Psalms 71:19; 86:8; 89:6, 8.)

What specifications of "the man of sin" are thus met?

"Let no man deceive you by any means: for that day shall not come, except there come a falling away first, and that man of sin be revealed, the son of perdition; *who opposeth and exalteth himself above all that is called God, or that is worshipped; so that he as God sitteth in the temple of God, shewing himself that he is God.*" 2 Thessalonians 2:3, 4.

What did Babylon give the nations to drink?

"She made all nations drink of *the wine of the wrath of her fornication.*" Revelation 14:8.

What are those to drink who accept the teachings of Babylon, and thus render homage to the beast?

"The same shall drink of *the wine of the wrath*

of God, which is poured out without mixture into the cup of his indignation." Verse 10.

NOTE.—The cup of the Lord, which contains the new covenant in the blood of Christ, and the cup of the wine of the wrath of Babylon are both offered to the world. To drink of the former, that is, to accept the true gospel, is to receive everlasting life; but to drink of the wine of Babylon, that is, to accept the false gospel taught by the Papacy, will result in drinking of the wine of the wrath of God from the cup of His indignation. The true gospel means everlasting life; the false gospel, everlasting death.

FALSE WORSHIP ENFORCED

Under what threatened penalty is the worship of the image of the beast enforced?

"And he had power to give life unto the image of the beast, that the image of the beast should both speak, and *cause [decree] that as many as would not worship the image of the beast should be killed.*" Revelation 13:15.

NOTE.—For an explanation of the image of the beast, see reading on "The Dragon's Voice Heard Again," page 87.

What universal boycott is to be employed in an attempt to compel all to receive the mark of the beast?

"And he causeth all, both small and great, rich and poor, free and bond, to receive a mark in their right hand, or in their foreheads: and *that no man might buy or sell, save he that had the mark, or the name of the beast, or the number of his name.*" Verses 16, 17.

NOTE.—Regarding the mark of the beast, see reading on "Sunday Law Advocate," page 87.

SATAN, OR GOD?

Who is the real power operating through the beast?

"The *dragon* gave him his power, and his seat, and great authority." Verse 2.

Who is this dragon?

"And the great dragon was cast out, that old serpent, called the *Devil,* and *Satan,* which deceiveth the whole world." Revelation 12:9.

How did the devil seek to induce Jesus to worship him?

"And the devil, taking him up into an high mountain, shewed unto him all the kingdoms of the world in a moment of time. And the devil said unto him, *All this power will I give thee,* and the glory of them: for that is delivered unto me; and to whomsoever I will I give it. *If thou therefore wilt worship me, all shall be thine.*" Luke 4:5-7.

How did Jesus show His loyalty to God?

"And Jesus answered and said unto him, *Get thee behind me, Satan: for it is written, Thou shalt worship the Lord thy God, and him only shalt thou serve.*" Verse 8.

NOTE.—The threefold message of Revelation 14: 6-12 is proclaimed in connection with the closing scenes of the great controversy between Christ and Satan. Lucifer has sought to put himself in the place of God (Isaiah 14:12-14), and to secure to himself the worship that is due God alone. The final test comes over the commandments of God. Those who acknowledge the supremacy of the beast by yielding obedience to the law of God as changed and enforced by the Papacy, when the real issue has been clearly defined, will, in so doing, worship the beast and his image, and receive his mark. Such will take the side of Satan in his rebellion against God's authority.

THE TEN-HORNED BEAST OF REVELATION 13

What is the first symbol of Revelation 13?

"And I stood upon the sand of the sea, and saw *a beast rise up out of the sea, having seven heads and ten horns,* and upon his horns ten crowns, and upon his heads the name of blasphemy." Revelation 13:1.

NOTE.—As already learned from studying the Book of Daniel, a beast in prophecy represents some great earthly power or kingdom; a head or horn, a governing power; waters, "peoples, and multitudes, and nations, and tongues." (Revelation 17:15.)

"The beasts of Daniel and John are empires. The ten-horned beast is the Roman power. . . . The head is the governing power in the body. The heads of this beast represent successive governments."—H. GRATTAN GUINNESS, *Romanism and the Reformation*, pp. 144, 145.

How is this beast further described?

"And the beast which I saw was *like unto a leopard,* and his feet were as *the feet of a bear,* and his mouth *as the mouth of a lion.*" Revelation 13:2.

NOTE.—These are the characteristics of the first three symbols of Daniel 7—the *lion, bear,* and *leopard* there representing the kingdoms of *Babylon, Persia,* and *Greece*—and suggest this beast as representing or belonging to the kingdom symbolized by the *fourth beast* of Daniel 7, or *Rome.* Both have ten horns. Like the dragon of Revelation 12, it also has seven heads; but as the dragon symbolized Rome in its entirety, particularly in its pagan phase, this, like the "little horn" coming up among the ten horns of the fourth beast of Daniel 7, represents Rome in its later or papal form. Both it and the little horn have "a mouth" speaking great things; both make war upon the saints; both continue for the same period.

Allowing a very broad meaning to the symbol, the Douay Version, or English Catholic Bible, in a

note on Revelation 13:1, explains the seven heads of this beast as follows: "The seven heads are seven kings, that is, seven principal kingdoms or empires, which have exercised, or shall exercise, tyrannical power over the people of God: of these, five were then fallen, viz., the Egyptian, Assyrian, Chaldean, Persian, and Grecian monarchies; one was present, viz., the empire of Rome; and the seventh and chiefest was to come, viz., the great Antichrist and his empire." That the seventh head represents antichrist, or the Papacy, there can be little doubt.

THE DRAGON GIVES PLACE TO THE BEAST

What did the dragon give this beast?

"And the dragon gave him his *power,* and his *seat,* and *great authority.*" Verse 2.

NOTE.—It is an undisputed fact of history that under the later Roman emperors, after Constantine, the religion of the Roman government was changed from pagan to papal; that the bishops of Rome received rich gifts and great authority from Constantine and succeeding emperors; that after A.D. 476 the Bishop of Rome became the most influential power in Western Rome, and by Justinian, in 533, was declared "head of all the holy churches," and "corrector of heretics." (See note on page 173.) "The removal of the capital of the Empire from Rome to Constantinople in 330, left the Western Church, practically free from imperial power, to develop its own form of organisation. The Bishop of Rome, *in the seat of the Caesars,* was now the greatest man in the West, and was soon [when the barbarians overran the empire] forced to become the political as well as the spiritual head."—A. C. FLICK, *The Rise of the Mediaeval Church* (Putnam's, 1909 ed.), p. 168.

Thus Rome pagan became Rome papal; church and state were united, and the persecuting power of the dragon was conferred upon the professed head of the church of Christ, or papal Rome. "The Pope, who calls himself 'King' and 'Pontifex Maximus,' is Caesar's successor."—ADOLPH HARNACK, *What Is Christianity?* (Putnam's, 1903 ed.), p. 270.

How are the character, work, period of supremacy, and great power of the beast described?

"And there was given unto him a mouth speaking great things and blasphemies; and power was given unto him to continue forty and two months. And he opened his mouth in blasphemy against God, to blaspheme his name, and his tabernacle, and them that dwell in heaven. And it was given unto him to make war with the saints, and to overcome them: and power was given him over all kindreds, and tongues, and nations." Verses 5-7.

NOTE.—All these specifications have been fully and accurately met in the Papacy, and identify this beast as representing the same power as the represented by the little-horn phase of the fourth beast of Daniel 7, and the little horn of Daniel 8, in its chief and essential features and work. (See Daniel 7:25; 8:11, 12, 24, 25, and readings on page 46 and 83. For an explanation of the time period mentioned, see page 83.)

THE BEAST RECEIVES A DEADLY WOUND

What was to happen to one of the heads of this beast?

"And I saw *one of his heads as it were wounded to death;* and his deadly wound was healed: and all the world wondered after the beast." Revelation 13:3.

> NOTE.—The "deadly wound" to the papal head of this beast was inflicted when the French, in 1798, entered Rome and took the pope prisoner, eclipsing, for a time, the power of the Papacy and depriving it of its temporalities. Again in 1870 temporal dominion was taken from the Papacy, and the pope looked upon himself as the prisoner of the Vatican. By 1929 the situation had changed to the extent that Cardinal Gasparri met Premier Mussolini in the historic palace of Saint John Lateran to settle a long quarrel—returning temporal power to the papacy, to "heal a wound of 59 years" (*The Catholic Advocate* [Australia], April 18, 1929, p. 16).
>
> The front page of the San Francisco *Chronicle* of February 12, 1929, carried pictures of Cardinal Gasparri and Mussolini, signers of the Concordat, with the headline "Heal Wound of Many Years." The Associated Press dispatch said: "In affixing the autographs to the memorable document, healing the wound which has festered since 1870, extreme cordiality was displayed on both sides." To such a position of influence over the nations is the Papacy finally to attain that just before her complete overthrow and destruction she will say, "I sit a queen, and am no widow, and shall see no sorrow." Revelation 18:7. (See Isaiah 47:7-15; Revelation 17:18.)

What is said of the Papacy's captivity and downfall?

"He that leadeth into captivity shall go into captivity: he that killeth with the sword must be killed with the sword." Revelation 13:10.

What questions indicate the high position of this beast-power?

"And they worshipped the dragon which gave power unto the beast: and they worshipped the beast, saying, *Who is like unto the beast? who is able to make war with him?*" Verse 4.

How universal is the worship of this power to become?

"And all that dwell upon the earth shall worship him, whose names are not written in the book of life of the Lamb slain from the foundation of the world." Verse 8.

THE BEAST DESTROYED

What did John say was to be the end of this beast?

"And the beast was taken, and with him the false prophet that wrought miracles before him. . . . *These both were cast alive into a lake of fire burning with brinstone.*" Revelation 19:20. (See Isaiah 47:7-15; 2 Thessalonians 2:3-8; Revelation 17: 16, 17; 18:4-8.)

What is the fate of the fourth beast of Daniel 7?

"I beheld then because of the voice of the great words which the horn spake: I beheld even till the beast was *slain,* and his body *destroyed,* and *given to the burning flame.*" Daniel 7:11.

ANOTHER BEAST APPEARS

When was the papal head of the first beast of Revelation 13 wounded?

In 1798, when the Papacy was temporarily overthrown by the French, under General Berthier. (See preceding reading.)

What did the prophet see coming up at this time?

"And I beheld *another beast coming up out of the earth;* and he had two horns like a lamb, and he spake as a dragon." Revelation 13:11.

> NOTE.—John Wesley, in his note on Revelation 13: 11, written in 1754, says of the two-horned beast: "He is not yet come: tho' he cannot be far off. For he is to appear at the End of the forty-two Months of the first Beast."—*Explanatory Notes Upon the New Testament* (1791 ed.), Vol. 3, p. 299.
>
> The previous beast came up out of the "sea," which indicates its rise among the peoples and nations of the world then in existence (Revelation 17:15), whereas this latter power comes up out of the "earth," where there had not before been "peoples, and multitudes, and nations, and tongues." In 1798, when the papal power received its deadly wound, the United States, located in the Western Hemisphere, was the only great world power then coming into prominence in territory not previously occupied by peoples, multitudes, and nations. Only nine years preceding this (in 1789), the United States adopted its national Constitution. It is within the territory of the United States, therefore, that we may look for a fulfillment of this prophecy.
>
> The eminent American preacher De Witt Talmage based a sermon, "America for God," on the text of Revelation 13:11, interpreting the beast with two horns like a lamb as referring to the United States. "Is it reasonable," he said, "to suppose that God would leave out from the prophecies of his Book this whole Western Hemisphere? No, No!" See his *500 Selected Sermons,* Vol. 2 (1900), p. 9.

What is the character of this new power?

"He had *two horns like a lamb.*" Verse 11.

NOTE.—How fittingly is the United States characterized in these words! The nations of the past, pictured in the Bible as beasts of prey, were filled with intolerance, persecution, and oppression. In sharp contrast, the United States was founded on the principles of liberty, equality, and tolerance. The men who had fled the tribulations of the Old World were determined that those trials should not be repeated in the New.

The principles of civil and religious liberty which have made the United States great were incorporated into the fundamental law of the nation at its very founding. We quote from the first amendments to the Constitution, commonly known as the Bill of Rights:

Article I. "Congress shall make no law respecting an establishment of religion, or prohibiting the free exercise thereof; or abridging the freedom of speech or of the press; or the right of the people peaceably to assemble, and to petition the government for a redress of grievances."

Article IV. "The right of the people to be secure in their persons, houses, papers, and effects, against unreasonable searches and seizures, shall not be violated."

Article V. "No person shall be . . . subject for the same offense to be twice put in jeopardy of life or limb, nor shall be compelled in any criminal case to be a witness against himself; nor to be deprived of life, liberty, or property, without due process of law; nor shall private property be taken for public use without just compensation."

For these principles men have fought and died. For them statesmen have valiantly contended throughout the nation's history. For these liberties, millions today are ready to sacrifice even life itself.

THE DRAGON'S VOICE HEARD AGAIN

Notwithstanding the lamblike appearance of this power, what will ultimately happen?

"And he *spake as a dragon.*" Verse 11.

NOTE.—The voice of the dragon is the voice of intolerance and persecution. It is repugnant to the American mind to think that religious persecution might mar the fair record of the nation founded on liberty to all. But all through the history of the country, from its very founding, farseeing statesmen have recognized that the tendency to enforce religious dogmas by civil law is all too common with mankind, and is likely to break out in active persecution in unexpected places unless specifically guarded against.

Said Thomas Jefferson, at the very beginning of the nation's existence: "The spirit of the times may alter, will alter. Our rulers will become corrupt, our people careless. A single zealot may commence persecution, and better men be his victims."—*Notes on Virginia*, Query XVII, in *The Works of Thomas Jefferson* (Ford ed., 1904-05), Vol. 4, pp. 81, 82.

In a letter to Rabbi Mordecai M. Noah, this same great American wrote: "Your sect by its sufferings has furnished a remarkable proof of the universal spirit of religious intolerance, inherent in every sect. . . . Our laws have applied the only antidote to the vice. . . . But more remains to be done; for although we are free by the law, we are not so in practice; public opinion erects itself into an Inquisition, and exercises its office with as much fanaticism as fans the flames of an auto da fe."—Letter to Mordecai

M. Noah, May 28, 1818, *Thomas Jefferson Papers*, Vol. 213, p. 37988, in Manuscript Division, Library of Congress.

To the honor of the nation, it should be said that noble statesmen have largely held in check the tendency which Thomas Jefferson foresaw working in the body politic. But no American can shut his eyes to the fact that paralleling these noble efforts, zealous efforts have been made by misguided religious leaders to secure civil enforcement of religious usages.

How much power will this beast exercise?

"And *he exerciseth all the power of the first beast before him,* and causeth the earth and them which dwell therein to worship the first beast, whose deadly wound was healed." Verse 12.

NOTE.—The "first beast before him"—papal Rome (see preceding reading)—exercised the power of persecuting all who differed with it in religious matters.

What means will be employed to lead the people back into false worship?

"And deceiveth them that dwell on the earth *by the means of those miracles which he had power to do* in the sight of the beast." Verse 14.

What will this power propose that the people shall do?

"Saying to them that dwell on the earth, *that they should make an image to the beast, which had the wound by a sword, and did live.*" Verse 14.

NOTE.—The beast "which had the wound by a sword, and did live," is the Papacy. That was a church dominating the civil power, a union of church and state, enforcing its religious dogmas by the civil power, by confiscation, imprisonment, and death. An image to this beast would be another ecclesiastical organization clothed with civil power—another union of church and state—to enforce religion by law.

SUNDAY LAW ADVOCATES

Does the history of the United States show that religious organizations have attempted to secure legislation involving religion?

Organizations such as the National Reform Association, the International Reform Federation, the Lord's Day Alliance of the United States, and the New York Sabbath Committee have for years worked to secure Sunday legislation. They have often secured the aid of civic groups.

What, according to its constitution, is an avowed object of the National Reform Association?

"To secure such an amendment to the Constitution of the United States as will . . . indicate that this is a Christian nation, and place all the Christian laws, institutions, and usages of our government on an undeniably legal basis in the fundamental law of the land."—DAVID MCALLISTER, *The National Reform Movement . . . a Manual of Christian Civil Government* (1898 ed.), "Article II of Constitution," pp. 15, 16.

NOTE.—A general superintendent of the National Reform Association and editor of the *Christian Statesman* propounded the following amendment to the First Amendment of the United States Constitution:

"How to take a most dangerous weapon out of the hands of secularists: Amend the highest written law of the land, our Federal Constitution, so that it shall plainly proclaim the will of the Lord of nations as the rule of our national life and the standard of our national conduct in dealing with all our problems —internal and external, national and international. As that Constitution now stands, the secularist is perpetually quoting it on his side, loudly proclaiming that there is in it nothing that warrants the Christian usages, and as loudly and persistently demanding that all these and their like shall go out of the latter that it may be brought into perfect harmony with the former. Our answer should be—Never! But we will instead change the written document that it may be in perfect harmony with the unwritten and so furnish an undeniably legal basis for all we have that is Christian in our national life and character and also for more of its kind that is still needed."— *Christian Statesman*, August, 1921, p. 25.

At first glance, such a statement as this might appear worthy of endorsement. But a closer examination reveals a reasoning basically the same as that employed by religious leaders of past ages, who persecuted all who differed with them. If the laws of the land should regulate religious observances, a man could be forced to attend church, to be baptized, or to pay for the support of the clergy.

What has this association said on this point regarding the Catholic Church?

"We cordially, gladly, recognize the fact that in South American Republics, and in France and other European countries, the Roman Catholics are the recognized advocates of national Christianity, and stand opposed to all the proposals of secularism. . . . *Whenever they are willing to cooperate in resisting the progress of political atheism, we will gladly join hands with them* in a World's Conference for the promotion of National Christianity—which ought to be held at no distant day—many countries could be represented only by Roman Catholics."—Editorial, *Christian Statesman* (official organ of the National Reform Association), Dec. 11, 1884, p. 2.

What has the pope commanded all Catholics to do in regard to government?

"First and foremost it is the duty of all Catholics worthy of the name and wishful to be known as the most loving children of the Church . . . to

endeavor to bring back all civil society to the pattern and form of Christianity which we have described."—*The Great Encyclical Letters of Leo XIII*, "Encyclical Letter *Immortale Dei*, Nov. 1, 1885," p. 132.

NOTE.—On September 7, 1947, Pope Pius XII declared that "'the time for reflection and planning is past' in religious and moral fields and the 'time for action' has arrived." He said that "the battle in religious and moral fields hinged on five points: Religious culture, *the sanctifying of Sunday*, the saving of the Christian family, social justice, and loyalty and truthfulness in dealings."—*Evening Star* (Washington, D.C.), Sept. 8, 1947.

On September 21, 1961, Pope John, in an audience with members of a labor union, asked for the proper observance of Sunday as a day of rest. Said the Pope, This "presupposes a change of mind in society and the *intervention of the powers of the state*."

What is the object of the International Reform Federation?

"The Reform Bureau [now Federation] is the first 'Christian lobby' established at our national capital to speak to government in behalf of all denominations."—*History of the International Reform Bureau* (1911), p. 2.

NOTE.—The securing of compulsory Sunday legislation is one of the chief objects of this and other like organizations. (See pages 60-62 of the above-named work.)

What is the object of the Lord's Day Alliance?

"This organization proposes in every possible way to aid in preserving Sunday as a *civil institution*. Our national security requires the active support of all good citizens in the maintenance of our American Sabbath. *Sunday laws must be enacted and enforced*."—Quoted as "principles contained in the Constitution" of the original organization (then called the American Sabbath Union); cited in *The Lord's Day Alliance, Twenty-fifth Annual Report* (1913), p. 6.

What was one of the first objectives stated by the Federal Council of the Churches of Christ in America (predecessor of the National Council of the Churches of Christ in the United States of America)?

"That all encroachments upon the claims and the sanctities of the Lord's Day should be *stoutly resisted* through the press, the Lord's Day associations and alliances, *and by such legislation as may be secured to protect and preserve this bulwark of our American Christianity*."—Resolution passed in the first meeting of the Federal Council of the Churches of Christ in America (1908), in its first *Biennial Report*, p. 103.

NOTE.—Thus it will be seen that the securing of laws for the enforcement of Sunday observance is a prominent feature in all these organizations in their efforts to "Christianize" the nation. In doing this many fail to see that they are repudiating the principles of Christianity, of Protestantism, and of the United States Constitution, and playing directly into the hand of that power which originated the Sunday sabbath—the Papacy.

What arguments have been offered for Sunday laws?

"That the day might be devoted with less interruption to the purposes of devotion." "That the devotion of the faithful might be free from all disturbance."—AUGUSTUS NEANDER, *General History of the Christian Religion and Church,* Torrey translation (3d American ed.), Vol. 2, p. 301.

NOTE.—In the fourth and fifth centuries, Sunday shows and Sunday theaters, it was complained, hindered the "devotion of the faithful," because many of the members attended them in preference to the church services. The church, therefore, demanded that the state should interfere and promote Sunday observance by law. "In this way," says Neander, "the church received help from the state for the furtherance of her ends."—*Ibid.,* pp. 300, 301. This union of church and state served to establish the Papacy in power. A similar course pursued now will produce the same results.

"On the baseless assumption that the seventh day, set apart and established in the law, has been in some way superseded by the first day, recognized in the gospel, a good deal of hurtful legislation has been enacted on the pretext of sanctifying the Sabbath and honoring God. Men who really do know better are willing to wrest the Scriptures and appeal to popular ignorance in order to gain a point. Such conduct is unworthy of any good cause.

"This error had its origin in the iniquitous union of church and state, and is a relic of that oppressive system. . . . In current usage the so-called Sabbath legislation does not apply to the Bible Sabbath at all, but to the first day of the week. The practical effect of such legislation generally is to annul the divine commandment, and to put in its place a human statute. The vicious assumption underlying such legislation is that divine law may be changed or amended by human enactment. In thousands of minds to-day the law of God concerning the Sabbath day is rendered of none effect by the so-called Sabbath legislation enacted by civil governments. Such legislation belittles the authority of Jehovah."—J. J. TAYLOR (Baptist), *The Sabbatic Question* (New York: Fleming H. Revell, 1914), pp. 51, 52, 58.

EARLY AND MODERN SUNDAY LAWS

Who is responsible for the present state Sunday laws of the United States?

"During nearly all our American history *the churches* have influenced the States to make and improve Sabbath laws."—W. F. CRAFTS, in *Christian Statesman,* July 3, 1890, p. 5.

NOTE.—These Sunday laws are a survival of the complete union of church and state which existed at the founding of the colonies. "Such laws [as the Maryland Sunday law of 1723] were the outgrowth of the system of religious intolerance that prevailed in many of the colonies."—Decision of Court of Appeals of the District of Columbia, Jan. 21, 1908, in *Washington Law Reporter,* Feb. 14, 1908, p. 103.

The first Sunday law imposed on an American colony (Virginia, 1610) required church attendance and prescribed the death penalty for the third offense. (See Peter Force, *Tracts Relating to the Colonies in North America* [1844 ed.], Vol. 3, No. 2, p. 11.)

Why is a national Sunday law demanded?

"National Sunday legislation is needed to make the state laws complete and effective," say its advocates.

NOTE.—The *state* laws enforcing a religious day are relics of a union of church and state in colonial times. But the *nation* whose foundation principles of civil and religious freedom are aptly symbolized by two lamblike horns does not exercise "all the power of the first beast" and require men "to worship the first beast, whose deadly wound was healed," until it abandons its separation of church and state to the extent of enforcing religious requirements on a national scale, thus constituting an "image," or likeness, to the first beast.

THE MARK OF PAPAL AUTHORITY

What does the prophet say this second ecclesiastico-political power will attempt to enforce upon all the people?

"And he causeth all, both small and great, rich and poor, free and bond, to receive *a mark* in their right hand, or in their foreheads." Revelation 13: 16.

NOTE.—This mark, called in verse 17 "the mark . . . of the beast," is set over against the seal of God in the Book of Revelation. (See Revelation 14:9, 10.)

What means will be employed to compel all to receive this mark?

"And *that no man might buy or sell, save he that had the mark,* or the name of the beast, or the number of his name." Revelation 13:17.

NOTE.—That is, all who refuse to receive this mark will be boycotted, or denied the rights and privileges of business and trade, or the ordinary means of gaining a livelihood.

Good News About
FINANCIAL SECURITY

GOD'S PORTION AND ITS PURPOSE

What is one way in which we are commanded to honor God?

"Honour the Lord *with thy substance,* and *with the firstfruits of all thine increase."* Proverbs 3:9.

What part of one's income has the Lord especially claimed as His?

"And *all the tithe [tenth] of the land,* whether of the seed of the land, or of the fruit of the tree, *is the Lord's: it is holy unto the Lord."* Leviticus 27:30.

For whose support and for what work was the tithe devoted in Israel?

"Behold, I have given *the children of Levi* all the tenth in Israel for an inheritance, *for their service which they serve, even the service of the tabernacle of the congregation."* Numbers 18:21.

How does Paul say gospel ministry is supported?

"If we have sown unto you spiritual things, is it a great thing if we shall reap your carnal things? . . . Do ye not know that they which minister about holy things live of the things of the temple? and they which wait at the altar are partakers with the altar? *Even so hath the Lord ordained that they which preach the gospel should live of the gospel."* 1 Corinthians 9:11-14.

FUNDAMENTAL BASIS OF TITHE PAYING

Upon what fundamental basis does the requirement of tithe paying rest?

"The earth is the Lord's, and the fullness thereof; the world, and they that dwell therein." Psalm 24:1.

Who is it that gives man power to get wealth on earth?

"But thou shalt remember the Lord thy God: for *it is he that giveth thee power to get wealth."* Deuteronomy 8:18.

What statement of Christ shows that man is not an original owner, but a steward of God's goods?

"For the kingdom of heaven is as a man travelling into a far country, who called his own servants, and *delivered unto them his goods."* Matthew 25:14. (See 1 Corinthians 4:7.)

HISTORY OF TITHE PAYING

How early in the history of the world do we read of tithe paying?

"For this Melchisedec, king of Salem, priest of the most high God, who met Abraham returning from the slaughter of the kings, and blessed him; to whom also *Abraham gave a tenth part of all."* Hebrews 7:1, 2. (See Genesis 14:17-20.)

What vow did Jacob make at Bethel?

"And Jacob vowed a vow, saying, If God will be with me, and will keep me in this way that I go, and will give me bread to eat, and raiment to put on, so that I come again to my father's house in peace; then shall the Lord be my God: . . . and *of all that thou shalt give me I will surely give the tenth unto thee."* Genesis 28:20-22.

CURSE OR BLESSING

Of what is one guilty who withholds the tithe and freewill offerings?

"Will a man rob God? Yet *ye have robbed me.* But ye say, Wherein have we robbed Thee? *In tithes and offerings."* Malachi 3:8.

Concerning what does the Lord ask us to prove Him, and upon what conditions does He promise great blessings?

"Bring ye all the tithes into the storehouse, that there may be meat in mine house, *and prove me now herewith,* saith the Lord of hosts, if I will not open you the windows of heaven, and pour you out a blessing, that there shall not be room enough to receive it. And I will rebuke the devourer for your sakes, and he shall not destroy the fruits of your ground; neither shall your vine cast her fruit before the time in the field, saith the Lord of hosts." Verses 10, 11.

FINANCIAL SECURITY

A DISTINCTION IN TITHES AND OFFERINGS

By what has God ordained that His work be sustained?

"Tithes and offerings." Malachi 3:8.

How are we told to come into His courts?

"Bring an offering, and come into his courts." Psalm 96:8.

> NOTE—Various offerings are mentioned in the Bible, such as thank offerings, peace offerings, sin offerings, and trespass offerings.

Concerning the celebration of the three annual feasts, what instruction did God give to His people anciently?

"Three times thou shalt keep a feast unto me in the year. . . . And *none shall appear before me empty."* Exodus 23:14, 15.

ACCEPTABLE OFFERINGS

With what spirit would God have us give?

"Every man according as he purposeth in his heart, so let him give; not grudgingly, or of necessity: for *God loveth a cheerful giver."* 2 Corinthians 9:7.

What has Christ said regarding giving?

"It is *more blessed to give than to receive."* Acts 20:35.

According to what rule were the Israelites commanded to give?

"Every man shall give as he is able, according to the blessing of the Lord thy God which he hath given thee." Deuteronomy 16:17. (Compare 1 Corinthians 16:2.)

Upon what basis are gifts acceptable to God?

"For if there be first a willing mind, *it is accepted according to that a man hath,* and not according to that he hath not." 2 Corinthians 8:12.

What charge was Timothy instructed to give the rich?

"Charge them that are rich in this world, that they be not highminded, nor trust in uncertain riches, but in the living God, who giveth us richly all things to enjoy; *that they do good, that they be rich in good works, ready to distribute, willing to communicate;* laying up in store for themselves a good foundation against the time to come, that they may lay hold on eternal life." 1 Timothy 6:17-19.

How does God regard such a course?

"But to do good and to communicate ["share what you have," R.S.V.] forget not: for *with such sacrifices God is well pleased."* Hebrews 13:16.

THE CASE OF THE COVETOUS MAN

How does God regard the covetous man?

"The wicked boasteth of his heart's desire, and blesseth the covetous, *whom the Lord abhorreth."* Psalm 10:3. (See Exodus 18:21.)

What warning did Christ give against covetousness?

"Take heed, and *beware of covetousness:* for a man's life consisteth not in the abundance of the things which he possesseth." Luke 12:15.

How, in the parable, did God regard the selfish rich man?

"But God said unto him, *Thou fool,* this night thy soul shall be required of thee: then whose shall those things be, which thou hast provided?" Verse 20.

What application does Christ make of this parable?

"So is he that layeth up treasure for himself, and is not rich toward God." Verse 21. (See 1 Timothy 6:7.)

LAYING UP TREASURES IN HEAVEN

By what means can men lay up treasure in heaven?

"Sell that ye have, and give alms; provide yourselves bags which wax not old, a treasure in the heavens that faileth not, where no thief approacheth, neither moth corrupteth." Luke 12:33. (See 1 Timothy 6:7.)

What indicates where our hearts are?

"For *where your treasure is,* there will your heart be also." Luke 12:34.

Good News About
VIBRANT HEALTH

What did the apostle John wish concerning Gaius?

"Beloved, I wish above all things *that thou mayest prosper and be in health,* even as thy soul prospereth." 3 John 2.

What did God promise His people anciently?

"And ye shall serve the Lord your God, and he shall bless thy bread, and thy water; and *I will take sickness away from the midst of thee."* Exodus 23:25.

Upon what conditions was freedom from disease promised?

"If thou wilt diligently hearken to the voice of the Lord thy God, and wilt do that which is right in his sight, and wilt give ear to his commandments, and keep all his statutes, I will put none of these diseases upon thee, which I have brought upon the Egyptians: for I am the Lord that healeth thee." Exodus 15:26.

What does the psalmist say the Lord does for His people?

"Who forgiveth all thine iniquities; *who healeth all thy diseases."* Psalm 103:3.

What constituted a large part of Christ's ministry?

"Who went about doing good, and *healing all that were oppressed of the devil."* Acts 10:38. (See Luke 13:16.) "And Jesus went about all Galilee, . . . *healing all manner of sickness and all manner of disease among the people."* Matthew 4:23.

THE BIBLE SPEAKS OF OUR BODIES

Why should the health of the body be preserved?

"For ye are bought with a price: therefore *glorify God in your body,* and in your spirit, which are God's." 1 Corinthians 6:20.

What is the body of the believer said to be?

"What? know ye not that *your body is the temple of the Holy Ghost* which is in you, which ye have of God, and ye are not your own?" Verse 19.

FOOD PRINCIPLES—NOT FOOD FADS

What example did Daniel set in this matter?

"But Daniel purposed in his heart *that he would*

not defile himself with the portion of the king's meat, nor with the wine which he drank." Daniel 1:8.

With what food did he ask to be provided?

"Prove thy servants, I beseech thee, ten days; and *let them give us pulse [i.e., vegetables] to eat, and water to drink."* Verse 12.

What was the original diet prescribed for man?

"And God said, Behold, I have given you *every herb bearing seed,* which is upon the face of all the earth, and *every tree, in the which is the fruit of a tree yielding seed;* to you it shall be for meat." Genesis 1:29.

Why did the Lord restrict the Hebrews in their diet?

"For *thou art an holy people unto the Lord thy God, and the Lord hath chosen thee to be a peculiar people unto himself,* above all the nations that are upon the earth. Thou shalt not eat any abominable thing." Deuteronomy 14:2, 3.

NOTE—Both mind and body are affected by the food we eat.

REST, CHEER, AND HIGH PURPOSE

What effect does cheerfulness have upon the health?

"A merry heart *doeth good* like a medicine." Proverbs 17:22.

How did the Saviour provide rest for His disciples?

"And he said unto them, Come ye yourselves apart into a desert place, and *rest a while."* Mark 6:31.

How are we exhorted to present our bodies to God?

"I beseech you . . . that *ye present your bodies a living sacrifice, holy, acceptable unto God."* Romans 12:1.

What should control our habits of life?

"Whether therefore ye eat, or drink, or whatsoever ye do, *do all to the glory of God."* 1 Corinthians 10:31.

THE NATURE AND NECESSITY OF TEMPERANCE

Concerning what did Paul reason before Felix?

"He reasoned of righteousness, *temperance,* and judgment to come." Acts 24:25.

NOTE—Temperance means habitual moderation and control in the indulgence of the appetites and passions; in other words, self-control.

Of what is temperance a fruit?

"But *the fruit of the Spirit* is love, joy, peace, long-suffering, gentleness, goodness, faith, meekness, *temperance."* Galatians 5:22, 23.

NOTE—"Temperance puts wood on the fire, meal in the barrel, flour in the tub, money in the purse, credit in the country, contentment in the house, clothes on the back, and vigor in the body."—BENJAMIN FRANKLIN.

Where in Christian growth and experience is temperance placed by the apostle Peter?

"Add to your faith virtue; and to virtue knowledge; and to knowledge temperance; and to *temperance* patience; and to patience godliness; and to godliness brotherly kindness; and to brotherly kindness charity." 2 Peter 1:5-7.

NOTE—Temperance is rightly placed here as to order. Knowledge is a prerequisite to temperance, and temperance to patience. It is very difficult for an intemperate person to be patient.

What is said of those who strive for the mastery?

"And every man that striveth for the mastery is *temperate in all things."* 1 Corinthians 9:25.

THE BODY AND SELF-CONTROL

In running the Christian race, what did Paul say he did?

"But *I keep under my body, and bring it into subjection:* lest that by any means, when I have preached to others, I myself should be a castaway." Verse 27.

Why are kings and rulers admonished to be temperate?

"It is not for kings to drink wine; nor for princes strong drink: lest they drink, and *forget the law, and pervert the judgment of any of the afflicted."* Proverbs 31:4, 5.

Why were priests forbidden to use intoxicating drink while engaged in the sanctuary service?

"And the Lord spake unto Aaron, saying, Do not drink wine nor strong drink, thou, nor thy sons with thee, when ye go into the tabernacle . . . *that ye may put difference between holy and unholy, and between unclean and clean."* Leviticus 10:8-10.

Why is indulgence in strong drink dangerous?

"And be not drunk with wine, *wherein is excess;* but be filled with the Spirit." Ephesians 5:18.

For what should men eat and drink?

"Blessed art thou, O land, when thy king is the son of nobles, and thy princes eat in due season, *for strength,* and not for drunkenness!" Ecclesiastes 10:17.

GOD'S EARLY INSTRUCTION ON DIET

What was the original food provided for man?

"And God said, Behold, I have given you every *herb* bearing *seed,* which is upon the face of all the earth, and every tree, in the which is *the fruit of a tree* yielding *seed;* to you it shall be for meat." Genesis 1:29.

NOTE—In other words, vegetables, grains, fruits, and nuts.

After the Flood what other food was indicated as permissible?

"Every moving thing that liveth shall be meat for you; even as the green herb have I given you all things." Genesis 9:3.

NOTE—From this it is evident that flesh food was not included in the original diet provided for man, but that because of the changed conditions resulting from the Fall and the Flood, its use was permitted. However, Noah understood the difference between the clean and unclean animals, and a larger number of the clean beasts were housed safely in the ark. See Genesis 7:2.

FOUR FEARLESS YOUTH TEST TEMPERANCE

Why did Daniel refuse the food and wine of the king?

"But Daniel purposed in his heart *that he would not defile himself* with the portion of the king's meat, nor with the wine which he drank." Daniel 1:8. (See Judges 13:4.)

Instead of these, what did he request?

"Prove thy servants, I beseech thee, ten days; and let them give us *pulse [i.e., vegetables] to eat,* and *water to drink."* Verse 12.

At the end of ten days' test, how did he and his companions appear?

"And at the end of ten days their countenances appeared *fairer and fatter in flesh than all the children which did eat the portion of the king's meat."* Verse 15.

At the end of their three years' course in the school of Babylon, how did the wisdom of Daniel and his companions compare with that of others?

"Now at the end of the days . . . the king communed with them; *and among them all was found none like Daniel, Hananiah, Mishael, and Azariah: . . . and in all matters of wisdom and understanding, that the king enquired of them, he found them ten times better than all the magicians and astrologers that were in all his realm."* Verses 18-20.

BEGINNING AND END OF DRUNKARDS

What warning is given against leading others into intemperance?

"Woe unto him that giveth his neighbour drink, that puttest thy bottle to him, and makest him drunken." Habakkuk 2:15.

What kind of professed Christians are not fellowshiped?

"But now I have written unto you not to keep company, if any man that is called a brother be a fornicator, or covetous, or an idolater, or a railer, or a *drunkard."* 1 Corinthians 5:11.

Can drunkards enter the kingdom of God?

"Neither fornicators, nor idolaters, . . . nor thieves, nor covetous, nor *drunkards,* nor revilers, nor extortioners, shall inherit the kingdom of God." 1 Corinthians 6:9, 10. (See Revelation 21:27.)

For what did Paul pray?

"And the very God of peace sanctify you wholly; and I pray God *your whole spirit and soul and body be preserved blameless* unto the coming of our Lord Jesus Christ." 1 Thessalonians 5:23.

NOTE—For notable examples of total abstinence in the Bible, see the wife of Manoah, the mother of Samson (Judges 13:4, 12-14); Hannah, the mother of Samuel (1 Samuel 1:15); the Rechabites (Jeremiah 35:1-10); and John the Baptist (Luke 1:13-15).

Sacred Admonitions
A RESPONSIVE READING

"And the Lord spake unto Aaron, saying, Do not drink wine nor strong drink, thou, nor thy sons with thee." Leviticus 10:8, 9.

"He that loveth pleasure shall be a poor man: he that loveth wine and oil shall not be rich." Proverbs 21:17.

"For the drunkard and the glutton shall come to poverty: and drowsiness shall clothe a man with rags." Proverbs 23:21.

"Woe unto him that giveth his neighbour drink, that puttest thy bottle to him, and makest him drunken also." Habakkuk 2:15.

"Woe unto them that are mighty to drink wine, and men of strength to mingle strong drink." Isaiah 5:22.

"Be not drunk with wine, wherein is excess; but be filled with the Spirit." Ephesians 5:18.

"Wine is a mocker, strong drink is raging: and whosoever is deceived thereby is not wise." Proverbs 20:1.

"Who hath woe? who hath sorrow? who hath contentions? who hath babbling? who hath wounds without cause? who hath redness of eyes?" Proverbs 23:29.

"They that tarry long at the wine; they that go to seek mixed wine." Verse 30.

"Look not thou upon the wine when it is red, when it giveth his colour in the cup, when it moveth itself aright." Verse 31.

"At the last it biteth like a serpent, and stingeth like an adder." Verse 32.

"Be not deceived: neither fornicators, nor idolaters, nor adulterers, . . . nor thieves, nor covetous, nor drunkards, nor revilers, nor extortioners, shall inherit the kingdom of God." 1 Corinthians 6:9, 10.

"Now therefore beware, I pray thee, and drink not wine nor strong drink, and eat not any unclean thing." Judges 13:4.

"Know ye not that your body is the temple of the Holy Ghost which is in you, which ye have of God, and ye are not your own?" 1 Corinthians 6:19.

"For ye are bought with a price: therefore glorify God in your body, and in your spirit, which are God's." Verse 20.

"Whether therefore ye eat, or drink, or whatsoever ye do, do all to the glory of God." 1 Corinthians 10:31.

Good News About
THE COMFORTER

THE COMFORTER

What precious promise did Jesus make to His disciples shortly before His crucifixion?

"I will pray the Father, and *he shall give you another Comforter,* that he may abide with you for ever." John 14:16.

Why was it necessary for Christ to go away?

"Nevertheless I tell you the truth; It is expedient for you that I go away: for *if I go not away, the Comforter will not come unto you;* but if I depart, I will send him unto you." John 16:7.

Who is the Comforter, and what was He to do?

"But the Comforter, even the Holy Spirit, whom the Father will send in my name, *he shall teach you all things,* and bring to your remembrance all that I said unto you." John 14:26, RV.

What other work was the Comforter to do?

"And when he is come, he will reprove [literally, *"convince"]* the world of *sin,* and of *righteousness,* and of *judgment."* John 16:8.

THE SPIRIT OF TRUTH

By what other title is the Comforter designated?

"But when the Comforter is come, whom I will send unto you from the Father, even the *Spirit of truth,* which proceedeth from the Father, he shall testify of me." John 15:26.

What did Jesus say the Spirit of truth would do?

"Howbeit when he, the Spirit of truth, is come, *he will guide you into all truth:* for he shall not speak of himself; but whatsoever he shall hear, that shall he speak: and *he will shew you things to come."* John 16:13.

NOTE—The Spirit *speaks* (1 Timothy 4:1); *teaches* (1 Corinthians 2:13; *bears witness* (Romans 8:16); *makes intercession* (Romans 8:26); *distributes the gifts* (1 Corinthians 12:11); and *invites the sinner* (Revelation 22:17).

Why cannot the world receive Him?

"Even the Spirit of truth; whom the world cannot receive, *because it seeth him not, neither knoweth him."* John 14:17.

What did Christ say the Holy Spirit would reveal?

"He shall glorify *me:* for he shall *receive of mine,* and shall shew it unto you." John 16:14.

NOTE—It is plain from these scriptures that the Holy Spirit is the personal representative of Christ upon the earth, abiding in the church by dwelling in the hearts of the believers. It follows that any attempt to make a man the vicegerent of Christ in the place of the third person of the Godhead is an attempt to put man in the place of God. Thus does the fundamental principle of the Papacy set aside the person and the work of the Holy Spirit.

How has God revealed to us the hidden things of the kingdom?

"But God hath revealed them unto us *by his Spirit:* for the Spirit searcheth all things, yea, the deep things of God." 1 Corinthians 2:10.

Who moved upon the prophets to give their messages?

"For the prophecy came not in old time by the will of man: but holy men of God spake as they were moved by *the Holy Ghost."* 2 Peter 1:21.

After Pentecost, how was the gospel preached?

"With the Holy Ghost sent down from heaven." 1 Peter 1:12.

HEAVEN'S UNION WITH BELIEVERS

How intimate is His union with believers?

"But ye know him; for *he dwelleth with you,* and shall be in you." John 14:17.

Whose presence does the Holy Spirit bring to the believers?

"I will not leave you comfortless: *I will come to you."* Verse 18.

What promise is thus fulfilled?

"Lo, *I am with you alway,* even unto the end of the world." Matthew 28:20. (See also John 14:21-23.)

What threefold union is thus established as the result of belief in Christ?

"At that day ye shall know that *I am in my Father,* and *ye in me,* and *I in you."* John 14:20.

NOTE—Romans 8:9 shows the spirit of each of the three Persons of the Godhead to be one and the same spirit.

WARNING

What warning is therefore given?

"Grieve not the holy Spirit of God, whereby ye are sealed unto the day of redemption." Ephesians 4:30.

Is there a limit to the strivings of God's Spirit?

"And the Lord said, My Spirit shall not always strive with man." Genesis 6:3.

NOTE—The limit is determined by the creature rather than by the Creator. It is when there is an utter abandonment to evil, and further appeals would be without avail. God, foreknowing all things, may designate a definite period of probation for man, as in the case of the 120 years before the Flood (Genesis 6:3); but His Spirit never ceases to strive with man as long as there is hope of his salvation.

For what did David pray?

"Cast me not away from thy presence; and *take not thy holy spirit from me."* Psalm 51:11.

HEAVEN'S WILLINGNESS AND INVITATION

How willing is God to give us the Holy Spirit?

"If ye then, being evil, know how to give good gifts unto your children: how much more shall your heavenly Father give the Holy Spirit to them that ask him?" Luke 11:13.

How does Jesus, through the Spirit, seek an entrance to every heart?

"Behold, *I stand at the door, and knock:* if any man hear my voice, and open the door, I will come in to him, and will sup with him, and he with me." Revelation 3:20.

What is the fruit of the Spirit?

"The fruit of the Spirit is love, joy, peace, longsuffering, gentleness, goodness, faith, meekness, temperance." Galatians 5:22, 23.

What are the works of the flesh?

"Now the works of the flesh are manifest, which are these; Adultery, fornication, uncleanness, lasciviousness, idolatry, witchcraft, hatred, variance, emulations, wrath, strife, seditions, heresies, envyings, murders, drunkenness, revellings, and such like." Verses 19-21.

NOTE—The evils here mentioned are a close parallel to the lists found in Matthew 15:18, 19; Mark 7:20-23; Romans 1:29-31; and 2 Timothy 3:1-5.

How may the works of the flesh be avoided?

"Walk in the Spirit, and ye shall not fulfil the lust of the flesh." Galatians 5:16.

THE FRUIT OF LOVE

By what is the love of God shed abroad in the heart?

"The love of God is shed abroad in our hearts *by the Holy Ghost* which is given unto us." Romans 5:5.

What is love declared to be?

"And above all these things put on love, which is *the bond of perfectness."* Colossians 3:14, RV.

By what does genuine faith work?

"For in Jesus Christ neither circumcision availeth any thing, nor uncircumcision; but *faith which worketh by love."* Galatians 5:6.

What does love do?

"Hatred stirreth up strifes; but *love covereth all sins."* Proverbs 10:12. "Have fervent charity among yourselves: for *charity shall cover the multitude of sins."* 1 Peter 4:8.

In what way does love manifest itself?

"Love suffereth long, and is kind; love envieth not; love vaunteth not itself, is not puffed up, doth not behave itself unseemly, seeketh not its own, is not provoked, taketh not account of evil." 1 Corinthians 13:4, 5, RV.

THE KINGDOM OF GOD

Of what does the kingdom of God consist?

"For the kingdom of God is not meat and drink; but *righteousness,* and *peace,* and *joy* in the Holy Ghost." Romans 14:17.

NOTE—It is the Christian's privilege to have righteousness, peace, and joy—a righteousness which is of God by faith (Romans 3:21, 22); a peace that passeth understanding (Philippians 4:7), which the world can neither give nor take away; and a joy that rejoices evermore (1 Thessalonians 5:16; Philippians 4:4).

GENTLENESS, GOODNESS, FAITH

What does God's gentleness do for us?

"Thy gentleness hath *made me great."* Psalm 18:35.

What spirit should we show toward others?

"And the servant of the Lord must not strive; but *be gentle unto all men."* 2 Timothy 2:24.

What does the goodness of God do?

"Or despisest thou the riches of his goodness and forbearance and longsuffering; not knowing that *the goodness of God leadeth thee to repentance?"* Romans 2:4.

How should we treat those who have wronged us?

"Dearly beloved, *avenge not yourselves,* but rather give place unto wrath: for it is written, Vengeance is mine; I will repay, saith the Lord. Therefore *if thine enemy hunger, feed him; if he thirst, give him drink: for in so doing thou shalt heap coals of fire on his head."* Romans 12:19, 20.

How does faith determine our standing with God?
"But *without faith it is impossible to please him:* for he that cometh to God must believe that he is, and that he is a rewarder of them that diligently seek him." Hebrews 11:6.

MEEKNESS AND TEMPERANCE

How does God regard the meek and quiet spirit?
"Whose adorning . . . let it be the hidden man of the heart, . . . even the ornament of *a meek and quiet spirit, which is in the sight of God of great price."* 1 Peter 3:3, 4.

In our Christian growth and experience, what is to accompany faith, courage, and knowledge?
"Add to your faith virtue; and to virtue knowledge; and to knowledge *temperance."* 2 Peter 1:5, 6.

NOTE—One of the briefest and best definitions of temperance is *self-control.* The word in the text means much more than mere abstinence from intoxicating drinks—the limited sense now frequently given to it. It means control, strength, power, or ascendancy over exciting and evil passions of all kinds. It denotes the self-rule which the overcomer or converted man has over the evil propensities of his nature. Commenting on this passage, Dr. Albert Barnes says: "The influences of the Holy Spirit on the heart make a man moderate in all indulgences; teach him to restrain his passions, and to govern himself."

How is he commended who controls his spirit?
"He that is slow to anger is better than the mighty; and *he that ruleth his spirit than he that taketh a city."* Proverbs 16:32.

FROM CONDEMNATION TO PEACE

What is said of all these different virtues?
"Against such there is no law." Galatians 5:23.

NOTE—The law condemns sin. But all these things, being virtues, are in harmony with the law. They are produced by the Spirit; and the law, which is spiritual, cannot, therefore, condemn them.

To what unity are Christians exhorted?
"Endeavouring to keep *the unity of the Spirit* in the bond of peace." Ephesians 4:3.

GIFTS FROM THE GODHEAD

Concerning what subject ought we to be informed?

"Now *concerning spiritual gifts,* brethren, I would not have you ignorant." 1 Corinthians 12:1.

When Christ ascended, what did He give to men?
"Wherefore he saith, When he ascended up on high, he led captivity captive [literally, "he led captives captive"], and *gave gifts unto men."* Ephesians 4:8.

What were these gifts that Christ gave to men?
"And he gave some, *apostles;* and some, *prophets;* and some, *evangelists;* and some, *pastors* and *teachers."* Verse 11.

How are these gifts elsewhere spoken of?
"And God hath set some in the church, first *apostles,* secondarily *prophets,* thirdly *teachers,* after that *miracles,* then *gifts of healings, helps, governments, diversities of tongues."* 1 Corinthians 12:28.

PURPOSE OF THE GIFTS

For what purpose were these gifts bestowed upon the church?
"For the perfecting of the saints, for the work of the ministry, for the edifying of the body of Christ: . . . that we henceforth be no more children, tossed to and fro, and carried about with every wind of doctrine, by the sleight of men, and cunning craftiness, whereby they lie in wait to deceive; but speaking the truth in love, may grow up into him in all things, which is the head, even Christ." Ephesians 4:12-15.

What result is to be obtained by the exercise of the gifts in the church?
"Till we all come in [literally *"into"] the unity of the faith,* and of the knowledge of the Son of God, *unto a perfect man,* unto the measure of the stature of the fulness of Christ." Verse 13.

How is unity preserved in the diversities of gifts?
"Now there are diversities of gifts, but the *same Spirit."* 1 Corinthians 12:4.

For what purpose is the manifestation of this one Spirit given?
"But the manifestation of the Spirit is given to every man *to profit withal.* For to one is given by the Spirit the word of *wisdom;* to another the word of *knowledge* by the same Spirit; to another *faith* by the same Spirit; to another the gifts of *healing* by the same Spirit; to another the *working of miracles;* to another *prophecy;* to another *discerning of spirits;* to another *divers kinds of tongues;* to another the *interpretation of tongues."* Verses 7-10.

Who controls the distribution of the gifts of the Spirit?

"But all these worketh that one and the *selfsame Spirit,* dividing to every man severally as he will." Verse 11.

Was it God's design that all should possess the same gifts?

"Are all apostles? are all prophets? are all teachers? are all workers of miracles? have all the gifts of healing? do all speak with tongues? do all interpret?" Verses 29, 30.

PERIOD OF THE GIFTS

Were the gifts of the Spirit to continue forever?

"Whether there be prophecies, *they shall be done away;* whether there be tongues, *they shall cease;* whether there be knowledge, *it shall be done away.*" 1 Corinthians 13:8, RV.

When will the gifts of the Spirit not be needed?

"When that which is perfect is come, then that which is in part shall be done away." Verse 10.

AVENUES OF COMMUNICATION

How did God communicate with man in Eden?

"And the Lord God *called unto Adam, and said unto him,* Where art thou?" Genesis 3:9.

Since the Fall, by what means has God generally made known His will to man?

"I have also spoken *by the prophets,* and I have multiplied visions, and used similitudes, *by the ministry of the prophets.*" Hosea 12:10.

What things belong to God, and what to us?

"The secret things belong unto the Lord our God: *but those things which are revealed* belong unto us and to our children for ever." Deuteronomy 29:29.

How fully and to whom does God reveal His purposes?

"Surely the Lord God will do *nothing,* but *he revealeth his secret unto his servants the prophets.*" Amos 3:7.

THE GIFT OF PROPHECY

How does the Lord reveal Himself to His prophets?

"If there be a prophet among you, I the Lord will make myself known unto him in a *vision,* and will speak unto him in a *dream.*" Numbers 12:6.

Under what influence did the prophets of old speak?

"For the prophecy came not in old time by the will of man: but holy men of God spake *as they were moved by the Holy Ghost.*" 2 Peter 1:21. (See 2 Samuel 23:2.)

How are both the origin of prophecy and the means of communicating it still further shown in God's plan?

"The Revelation of Jesus Christ, which God gave unto him, to shew unto his servants things which must shortly come to pass; and *he sent and signified it by his angel unto his servant John.*" Revelation 1:1.

What angel revealed to Daniel his visions and dreams?

"Whiles I was speaking in prayer, even the man *Gabriel,* whom I had seen in the vision at the beginning, being caused to fly swiftly, touched me about the time of the evening oblation And *he informed me, and talked with me, and said,* O Daniel, I am now come forth to give thee skill and understanding." Daniel 9:21, 22. (See also chapter 10, and Revelation 22:9, 10.)

What Spirit was in the prophets inditing their utterances?

"Of which salvation the prophets have enquired and searched diligently, who prophesied of the grace that should come unto you: searching what, or what manner of time *the Spirit of Christ which was in them,* did signify, when it testified beforehand the sufferings of Christ, and the glory that should follow." 1 Peter 1:10, 11.

How were the Lord's words to the prophets preserved?

"Daniel had a dream and visions of his head upon his bed: then *he wrote the dream,* and told the sum of the matters." Daniel 7:1. (See Jeremiah 51:60; Revelation 1:10, 11.)

By whom has God spoken to us in these last days?

"God, who at sundry times and in divers manners spake in time past unto the fathers by the prophets, hath in these last days spoken unto us *by his Son.*" Hebrews 1:1, 2.

What was one of the offices to be filled by the Messiah?

"The Lord thy God will raise up unto thee *a Prophet* from the midst of thee, of thy brethren, like unto me; unto him ye shall hearken." Deuteronomy 18:15.

FORETELLING THE FUTURE

Can the wise men of the world foretell the future?

"Daniel answered before the king, and said, The secret which the king hath demanded can neither wise men, enchanters, magicians, nor soothsayers, shew unto the king." Daniel 2:27, RV.

Who did Daniel say could reveal secrets?

"But *there is a God in heaven that revealeth secrets,* and maketh known to the king Nebuchadnezzar what shall be in the latter days." Verse 28.

How did the prophet Daniel acknowledge the insufficiency of human wisdom?

"As for me, this secret is not revealed to me for any wisdom that I have more than any living, but for their sakes that shall make known the interpretation to the king, and that thou mightest know the thoughts of thy heart." Verse 30.

After revealing and interpreting the dream, what did Daniel say?

"The great God hath made known to the king what shall come to pass *hereafter."* Verse 45.

How does God show His foreknowledge?

"Behold, the former things are come to pass, and *new things do I declare: before they spring forth I tell you of them."* Isaiah 42:9.

What was foretold through the prophet Joel?

"And it shall come to pass afterward, that I will pour out my spirit upon all flesh; and *your sons and your daughters shall prophesy, your old men shall dream dreams, your young men shall see visions."* Joel 2:28.

When did this prediction begin to be fulfilled?

"But this is that which was spoken by the prophet Joel; And it shall come to pass in the last days, saith God, I will pour out of my Spirit upon all flesh: and your sons and your daughters shall prophesy, and your young men shall see visions, and your old men shall dream dreams." Acts 2:16, 17.

PROPHETIC LEADERSHIP

What were some of the gifts Christ gave to His church?

"When he ascended up on high, he led captivity captive, and gave gifts unto men. . . . And he gave some, *apostles;* and some, *prophets;* and some, *evangelists;* and some, *pastors* and *teachers."* Ephesians 4:8-11.

By what means did God deliver and preserve Israel?

"By a prophet the Lord brought Israel out of Egypt, and *by a prophet* was he preserved." Hosea 12:13.

When Moses complained of his slowness of speech, what did God say Aaron should be to him?

"And he shall be thy *spokesman* unto the people: and he shall be, even he shall be to thee instead of *a mouth,* and thou shalt be to him instead of God." Exodus 4:16.

What did God afterward call Aaron?

"And the Lord said unto Moses, See, I have made thee a god to Pharaoh: and Aaron thy brother shall be *thy prophet."* Exodus 7:1.

TESTS OF TRUE AND FALSE PROPHETS

What is one test by which to detect false prophets?

"When a prophet speaketh in the name of the Lord, *if the thing follow not, nor come to pass,* that is the thing which the Lord hath not spoken, but the prophet hath spoken it presumptuously: thou shalt not be afraid of him." Deuteronomy 18:22.

What other test should be applied in determining the validity of the claims of a prophet?

"If there arise among you a prophet, or a dreamer of dreams, and giveth thee a sign or a wonder, and the sign or the wonder come to pass, whereof he spake unto thee, saying, *Let us go after other gods,* which thou hast not known, and *let us serve them;* thou shalt not hearken unto the words of that prophet, or that dreamer of dreams: for the Lord your God proveth you, to know whether ye love the Lord your God with all your heart and with all your soul. *Ye shall walk after the Lord your God, and fear him, and keep his commandments, and obey his voice* and ye shall serve him, and cleave unto him." Deuteronomy 13:1-4.

NOTE—From these scriptures it will be seen that, in the first place, if a prophet's words do not prove to be true, it is evidence that God has not sent that prophet. On the other hand, even though the thing predicted comes to pass, if the pretended prophet seeks to lead others to break God's commandments, this, regardless of all signs, should be positive evidence that he is not a true prophet.

What rule did Christ give for distinguishing between true and false prophets?

"By their fruits ye shall know them." Matthew 7:20.

ATTITUDE TOWARD GOD'S PROPHETS

How did God's prophets anciently use the words of former prophets in exhorting the people to obedience?

"Should ye not hear the words which the Lord hath cried by the former prophets, when Jerusalem was inhabited and in prosperity?" Zechariah 7:7.

What is the promised result of believing God's prophets?

"Believe in the Lord your God, so shall ye be established; *believe his prophets, so shall ye prosper."* 2 Chronicles 20:20.

What admonition is given regarding the gift of prophecy?

"Despise not prophesyings. Prove all things; hold fast that which is good." 1 Thessalonians 5:20, 21.

What will characterize the last, or remnant, church?

"And the dragon was wroth with the woman, and went to make war with the remnant of her seed, *which keep the commandments of God, and have the testimony of Jesus Christ."* Revelation 12:17.

What is the "testimony of Jesus"?

"The testimony of Jesus is the spirit of prophecy." Revelation 19:10. (See Revelation 1:9.)

What results when this gift is absent?

"Where there is no vision, *the people perish:* but he that keepeth the law, happy is he." Proverbs 29:18. (See also Psalm 74:9.)

PROMISE AND PREPARATION OF PENTECOST

For what did Christ, just before His ascension, tell His disciples to wait?

"And, behold, I send the promise of my Father upon you: but tarry ye in the city of Jerusalem, *until ye be endued with power from on high."* Luke 24:49.

With what did He say they would be baptized?

"Ye shall be baptized *with the Holy Ghost* not many days hence." Acts 1:5.

NOTE—John the Baptist had foretold this baptism. He said, "I indeed baptize you with water unto repentance: but he that cometh after me is mightier than I, whose shoes I am not worthy to bear: he shall baptize you with the Holy Ghost, and with fire." Matthew 3:11.

For what work was this baptism to prepare them?

"But ye shall receive power, after that the Holy Ghost is come upon you: and *ye shall be witnesses unto me* both in Jerusalem, and in all Judea, and in Samaria, and unto the uttermost part of the earth." Acts 1:8.

RESULTS OF PENTECOST

What were some of the results of the preaching of the gospel under the outpouring of the Spirit?

"Now when they heard this, *they were pricked in their heart,* and said, . . . Men and brethren, what shall we do? Then Peter said unto them, Repent, and be baptized every one of you in the name of Jesus Christ for the remission of sins, and ye shall receive

the gift of the Holy Ghost. . . . Then they that gladly received his word were baptized: *and the same day there were added unto them about three thousand souls."* Acts 2:37-41. "And by the hands of the apostles were many signs and wonders wrought among the people; . . . *and believers were the more added to the Lord,* multitudes both of men and women." Acts 5:12-14. "And the word of God increased; and *the number of the disciples multiplied in Jerusalem greatly;* and a great company of the priests were obedient to the faith." Acts 6:7.

How did persecution affect the preaching of the gospel?

"And at that time there was a great persecution against the church which was at Jerusalem; and they were all scattered abroad throughout the regions of Judea and Samaria, except the apostles. . . . Therefore *they that were scattered abroad went every where preaching the word."* Acts 8:1-4.

NOTE—"Persecution has only had a tendency to extend and establish the faith which it was designed to destroy. . . . There is no lesson which men have been so slow to learn as that to oppose and persecute men is the very way to confirm them in their opinions, and to spread their doctrines."—DR. ALBERT BARNES, on Acts 4:4.

A LATTER-DAY OUTPOURING

What prophecy was fulfilled in the Pentecostal outpouring of the Spirit in the time of the apostles?

"But Peter, standing up with the eleven, lifted up his voice, and said, . . . These are not drunken, as ye suppose. . . . But *this is that which was spoken by the prophet Joel;* And it shall come to pass in the last days, saith God, I will pour out of my Spirit upon all flesh: and your sons and your daughters shall prophesy, and your young men shall see visions, and your old men shall dream dreams: and on my servants and on my handmaidens I will pour out in those days of my Spirit; and they shall prophesy." Acts 2:14-18. (See Joel 2:28, 29.)

What expressions in the prophecy of Joel seem to imply a double fulfillment of this outpouring of the Spirit?

"Be glad then, ye children of Zion, and rejoice in the Lord your God: for he hath given you the *former rain* moderately, and he will cause to come down for you the rain, the *former rain,* and the *latter rain* in the first month." Joel 2:23. (See also Hosea 6:3.)

NOTE—In Palestine the early rains prepare the soil for the seed sowing, and the latter rains ripen the grain for the harvest. So the early outpouring of the Spirit prepared the world for the extensive sowing of the gospel seed, and the final outpouring will come to ripen the golden grain for the harvest of the earth, which Christ says is "the end of the world." Matthew 13:37-39; Revelation 14:14, 15.

For what are we told to pray in the time of the "latter rain"?

"Ask ye of the Lord rain in the time of the latter rain; so the Lord shall make bright clouds, and give them showers of rain, to every one grass in the field." Zechariah 10:1.

NOTE—Before the apostles received the baptism of the Spirit in the early rain on the day of Pentecost, they all "continued with one accord in prayer and supplication." Acts 1:14. During this time they confessed their faults, put away their differences, ceased their selfish ambitions and contentions for place and power, so that when the time for the outpouring came, "they were all with one accord in one place," ready for its reception. To be prepared for the final outpouring of the Spirit, all sin and selfish ambition must again be put away, and a like work of grace wrought upon the hearts of God's people.

THE CALL OF REVELATION'S ANGEL

How is the closing gospel work under the outpouring of the Spirit described by the revelator?

"After these things I saw another angel come down from heaven, having great power; and *the earth was lightened with his glory."* Revelation 18:1.

What does this angel say?

"And he cried mightily with a strong voice, saying, *Babylon the great is fallen, is fallen,* and is become the habitation of devils, and the hold of every foul spirit, and a cage of every unclean and hateful bird." Verse 2.

NOTE—The religious world will then be in much the same condition as was the Jewish nation after it had rejected Christ at His first advent. (See 2 Timothy 3:1-5.)

What did Peter on the day of Pentecost tell his hearers to do?

"And with many other words did he testify and exhort, saying, *Save yourselves from this untoward generation."* Acts 2:40.

What similar call and appeal will be made under the final outpouring of the Spirit?

"And I heard another voice from heaven, saying, *Come out of her, my people,* that ye be not partakers of her sins, and that ye receive not of her plagues. For her sins have reached unto heaven, and God hath remembered her iniquities." Revelation 18:4, 5.

NOTE—A great work will be accomplished in a short time under the final outpouring of the Spirit. Many voices all over the earth will sound the warning cry. Signs and wonders will be wrought by the believers, and, as at Pentecost, thousands will be converted in a day.

Those who fail to heed this final gospel call, like the unbelieving Jews, will be doomed to destruction. The seven last plagues will overtake them, as war, famine, death, and destruction overtook the Jews, who, not believing in Christ, failed to heed His call to flee, and shut themselves up in Jerusalem to their doom. Those who heed the call and separate themselves from sin and from sinners will be saved.

Good News About
FOLLOWING CHRIST

What offering did King Hezekiah command to be made when he reestablished the worship of the Temple, following a period of apostasy?

"And Hezekiah commanded to offer the *burnt offering* upon the altar. And when the burnt offering began, the song of the Lord began also with the trumpets, and with the instruments ordained by David king of Israel." 2 Chronicles 29:27.

How did Hezekiah interpret the meaning of this service to the people of Judah?

"Then Hezekiah answered and said, *Now ye have consecrated yourselves unto the Lord,* come near and bring sacrifices and thank offerings into the house of the Lord. And the congregation brought in sacrifices and thank offerings; and as many as were of a free heart burnt offerings." Verse 31.

NOTE—The morning and the evening burnt offering (Exodus 29:38-41) symbolized the daily consecration of the people to the Lord.

CALL TO CONTINUAL CONSECRATION

How does the apostle Paul urge this consecration upon all Christians?

"I beseech you therefore, brethren, by the mercies of God, that ye present your bodies a living sacrifice, holy, acceptable unto God, which is your reasonable service." Romans 12:1.

What is the sacrifice of praise declared to be?

"Through him then let us offer up a sacrifice of praise to God continually, that is, the fruit of lips which make confession to his name." Hebrews 13:15, RV.

How is the service of consecration to be carried forward by the Christian church?

"Ye also, as lively stones, are built up a spiritual house, an holy priesthood, *to offer up spiritual sacrifices,* acceptable to God by Jesus Christ." 1 Peter 2:5.

THE EXAMPLE OF JESUS

Who has set the example of complete consecration?

"And whosoever will be chief among you, let him be your servant: even as *the Son of man* came not to be ministered unto, but to minister, and to give his life a ransom for many." Matthew 20:27, 28.

What position has Jesus taken among His brethren?

"For whether is greater, he that sitteth at meat, or he that serveth? is not he that sitteth at meat? but *I am among you as he that serveth."* Luke 22:27.

In what does likeness to Christ consist?

"Let this *mind* be in you, which was also in Christ Jesus." Philippians 2:5.

What did Christ's spirit of meekness and consecration lead Him to do?

"But made himself of no reputation, and *took upon him the form of a servant,* and was made in the likeness of men." Verse 7.

To what extent did Christ humble Himself?

"And being found in fashion as a man, he humbled himself, and became obedient *unto death, even the death of the cross."* Verse 8.

CALL TO COMPLETE CONSECRATION

How does He exhort us to the same consecration?

"Take my yoke upon you, and learn of me; for I am meek and lowly in heart: and ye shall find rest unto your souls." Matthew 11:29.

What does He make the condition of discipleship?

"So likewise, whosoever he be of you that forsaketh not all that he hath, he cannot be my disciple." Luke 14:33.

What is proof that one does not belong to Christ?

"If any man have not the Spirit of Christ, he is none of his." Romans 8:9.

How should he walk who professes to abide in Christ?

"He that saith he abideth in him *ought himself also so to walk,* even as he walked." 1 John 2:6.

Do we belong to ourselves?

"Know ye not that . . . *ye are not your own?* for ye are bought with a price." 1 Corinthians 6:19, 20.

Our Saviour in Prayer
Jim Padgett, Artist

What are we therefore exhorted to do?

"Therefore *glorify God in your body, and in your spirit,* which are God's." Verse 20.

NOTE—Our time, strength, and means are God's, and should be given to His service.

Of what are the bodies of Christians the temple?

"What? know ye not that your body is *the temple of the Holy Ghost* which is in you, which ye have of God?" Verse 19.

When truly consecrated, for what is one ready?

"Also I heard the voice of the Lord, saying, Whom shall I send, and who will go for us? *Then said I, Here am I; send me.*" Isaiah 6:8.

How is this willingness for service otherwise expressed?

"Behold, as the eyes of servants look unto the hand of their masters, and as the eyes of a maiden unto the hand of her mistress; *so our eyes wait upon the Lord our God.*" Psalm 123:2.

WHAT DIFFERENCE DOES IT MAKE?

Does it matter what one believes, so long as he is sincere?

"God hath from the beginning chosen you to salvation through sanctification of the Spirit and *belief of the truth.*" 2 Thessalonians 2:13.

NOTE—Doctrine affects the *life.* Truth leads to life and God; error to death and destruction. No one would think of saying it matters not what *god* one worships, so long as he is sincere, any more than he would think of saying it matters not what one *eats* or *drinks,* so long as he *relishes* what he eats and drinks or what *road* he travels, so long as he *thinks* he is on the right road. Sincerity is a virtue; but it is not the test of sound doctrine. God wills that we shall know the *truth,* and He has made provision whereby we may *know what is truth.*

Did Joshua think it immaterial what god Israel served?

"Now therefore fear the Lord, and serve him in sincerity and in truth: and *put away the gods which your fathers served on the other side of the flood and in Egypt; and serve ye the Lord.* And if it seem evil unto you to serve the Lord, choose you this day whom ye will serve; whether the gods which your fathers served that were on the other side of the flood, or the gods of the Amorites, in whose land ye dwell: but as for me and my house, we will serve the Lord." Joshua 24:14, 15.

NOTE—The influence of all idolatrous worship is degrading. (See Romans 1:21-32; Numbers 15; 1 Corinthians 10:20; 1 John 5:21.)

What advice was given to Timothy while preparing for the gospel ministry?

"Till I come, give attendance to reading, to exhortation, to *doctrine.* . . . Take heed unto thyself, and unto the *doctrine.*" 1 Timothy 4:13-16.

What solemn charge was given him concerning his public work?

"I charge thee therefore before God, and the Lord Jesus Christ, who shall judge the quick and the dead at his appearing and his kingdom; *Preach the word; . . . reprove, rebuke, exhort with all longsuffering and doctrine.*" 2 Timothy 4:1, 2.

What similar instruction was given to Titus?

"But speak thou the things which become *sound doctrine:*" "in all things shewing thyself a pattern of good works: *in doctrine shewing uncorruptness,* gravity, sincerity." Titus 2:1, 7.

WARNING AGAINST FALSE DOCTRINES

Of what kind of doctrines should we beware?

"That we henceforth be no more children, tossed to and fro, and carried about with every *wind of doctrine.*" Ephesians 4:14. (See also Hebrews 13:9.)

What is a "wind of doctrine"?

"And the prophets shall become *wind,* and *the word is not in them.*" Jeremiah 5:13.

NOTE—Calling a doctrine a wind of doctrine does not make it such. That is a wind of doctrine which is not sustained by the Word of God.

What danger attends the teaching of false doctrine?

"Who concerning the truth have erred, saying that the resurrection is past already; and *overthrow the faith of some.*" 2 Timothy 2:18.

What kind of worship results from false teaching?

"*But in vain they do worship me,* teaching for doctrines the commandments of men." Matthew 15:9.

By what doctrines are some to be misled in the last days?

"Now the Spirit speaketh expressly, that in the latter times some shall depart from the faith, giving heed to seducing spirits, and *doctrines of devils.*" 1 Timothy 4:1. (See 2 Peter 2:1.)

To what would men turn their ears?

"*For the time will come when they will not endure sound doctrine;* but after their own lusts shall they heap to themselves teachers, having itching ears; *and they shall turn away their ears from the truth, and shall be turned unto fables.*" 2 Timothy 4:3, 4.

THE TEST OF TRUE AND FALSE

How may we determine the truthfulness of any doctrine?
"Prove all things; hold fast that which is good." 1 Thessalonians 5:21.

NOTE—The Bible is the test of all doctrine. Whatever does not harmonize and square with this, is not to be received. "There is but one standard of the everlastingly right and the everlastingly wrong, and that is the Bible."—T. DE WITT TALMAGE.

For what is all Scripture profitable?
"All scripture is given by inspiration of God, and is *profitable for doctrine."* 2 Timothy 3:16.

What will sound doctrine enable the faithful teacher to do?
"Holding fast the faithful word as he hath been taught, that he may be able *by sound doctrine both to exhort and to convince the gainsayers."* Titus 1:9.

OUR PERSONAL ATTITUDE TOWARD TRUTH

Who are the disciples of Jesus, and what gracious work does the truth do for those who receive it?
"If ye continue in my word, then are ye my disciples indeed; and *ye shall know the truth, and the truth shall make you free."* John 8:31, 32.

Through what are they to be sanctified?
"Sanctify them through *thy truth:* thy word is truth." John 17:17.

Can we close our ears to truth, and remain innocent before God?
"He that turneth away his ear from hearing the law, *even his prayer shall be abomination."* Proverbs 28:9.

What did Christ say of those who will to do God's will?
"If any man willeth to do his will, *he shall know of the teaching,* whether it be of God, or whether I speak from myself." John 7:17, R.V. (See also Psalm 25:9; John 8:12.)

RESULTS OF OUR CHOICE

What will God allow to come to those who reject truth?
"Because they received not the love of the truth, that they might be saved. And for this cause God shall send them *strong delusion,* that they should believe a lie: that they all might be damned who believed not the truth, but had pleasure in unrighteousness." 2 Thessalonians 2:10-12.

What fate awaits blind teachers and their followers?
"Let them alone: they be blind leaders of the blind. And if the blind lead the blind, *both shall fall into the ditch."* Matthew 15:14.

To whom will the gates of the heavenly city finally be opened?
"Open ye the gates, *that the righteous nation which keepeth the truth* may enter in." Isaiah 26:2. (See also Revelation 22:14.)

WALKING IN THE LIGHT

How important is it that we walk in the light when it comes to us?
"Walk while ye have the light, *lest darkness come upon you:* for he that walketh in darkness knoweth not whither he goeth." John 12:35.

NOTE—It is important to settle a plain question of duty at once, and not delay obedience under the excuse of waiting for more light. To do as did Balaam—ask God again concerning that which He has plainly and expressly spoken—is dangerous. Nor should we, like the unbelieving Jews, seek a sign from Heaven to convince us that we ought to obey the Written Word. Has God spoken? Is it His word? Then obey. Do not insult Heaven with the question whether it is right to obey. (See 1 Kings 22:1-36; Ezekiel 14:1-5.)

Upon what condition are we promised cleansing from sin?
"But if we walk in the light, as he is in the light, we have fellowship one with another, and the blood of Jesus Christ his Son cleanseth us from all sin." 1 John 1:7.

SOURCES OF LIGHT

Who is the light of the world?
"I am the light of the world: he that followeth me shall not walk in darkness, but shall have the light of life." John 8:12.

How are we to walk in Christ?
"As ye have therefore received Christ Jesus the Lord, so walk ye in him." Colossians 2:6.

What has God given to guide our feet aright in the path of truth and duty?
"Thy word is a lamp unto my feet, and a *light* unto my path." Psalm 119:105. (See Proverbs 6:23.)

What does the entrance of God's Word give?
"The entrance of thy words *giveth light;* it giveth understanding unto the simple." Psalm 119:130.

Who does Christ say will be blessed through the prophecies of the book of Revelation?

"Blessed is *he that readeth,* and *they that hear* the words of this prophecy, *and keep those things which are written therein."* Revelation 1:3.

NOTE—We are in the last days, in the generation that is to hear the final warning message contained in this book. (See Revelation 14:6-10; 18:1-5.)

MORE LIGHT FOR THE RIGHTEOUS

How long may the just expect increased light to shine upon their pathway?

"But the path of the just is as the shining light, *that shineth more and more unto the perfect day."* Proverbs 4:18.

NOTE—The more earnestly one desires to know the will of God, while living up to all the light he has, the more light and truth from God will shine upon his pathway. If light is sown for the righteous, such are the very ones who may expect advanced light to come to them, and to see new duties presented to them from a study of the Word of God.

How did God respond to Cornelius' sincerity of worship?

"He saw in a vision evidently about the ninth hour of the day *an angel of God coming in to him, and saying unto him, Cornelius.* And when he looked on him, he was afraid, and said, What is it, Lord? And he said unto him, Thy prayers and thine alms are come up for a memorial before God." Acts 10:3, 4.

Because Cornelius' ways pleased the Lord, was this evidence that he had nothing more to learn or do?

"And now send men to Joppa, and call for one Simon, whose surname is Peter: he lodgeth with one Simon a tanner, whose house is by the sea side: *he shall tell thee what thou oughtest to do."* Verses 5, 6.

NOTE—The reason why the Lord favored Cornelius with a visit from one of His angels was not because Cornelius knew the way of salvation perfectly, but because the Lord saw in him a sincere desire for more light and a willing mind to comply with every known requirement. That spirit was

pleasing to God. All may now receive advanced light if, like Cornelius, they seek it and are willing to walk in it when it comes to them. If it is neglected, they are guilty before God and will be left to the buffetings of the enemy.

RESULTS OF OUR CHOICE

What will become of the light which one has if he fails to walk in it?

"The light of the body is the eye: therefore when thine eye is single, thy whole body also is full of light; but when thine eye is evil, thy body also is full of darkness. *Take heed therefore that the light which is in thee be not darkness."* Luke 11:34, 35.

Why are those condemned that do not come to the light?

"And this is the condemnation, that light is come into the world, and *men loved darkness rather than light, because their deeds were evil."* John 3:19.

If one is really seeking for truth, what will he do?

"But he that doeth truth *cometh to the light,* that his deeds may be made manifest, that they are wrought in God." Verse 21.

What will those who reject light and truth finally be led to believe?

"And for this cause God shall send them strong delusion, *that they should believe a lie:* that they all might be damned who believed not the truth, but had pleasure in unrighteousness." 2 Thessalonians 2:11, 12.

NOTE—The opposite of light is darkness; the opposite of truth is a lie. For those who reject light and truth, only darkness and error remain. God is sometimes in the Scriptures represented as sending that which He permits to come.

Upon what condition only may we be made partakers of Christ?

"For we are made partakers of Christ, *if we hold the beginning of our confidence stedfast unto the end."* Hebrews 3:14.

INDEX

FOR SCHOOL-AGE CHILDREN
The Bible Story
This is the most accurate and complete set of children's Bible story books available. More than 400 Bible stories are included, with full color paintings at every page-opening. Unlike television, these stories introduce children to heroes you would be proud to have them imitate. These stories are also an excellent tool for loving parents who want their children to grow up making right decisions and making them with confidence. Ten volumes, hardcover.

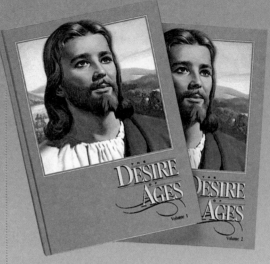

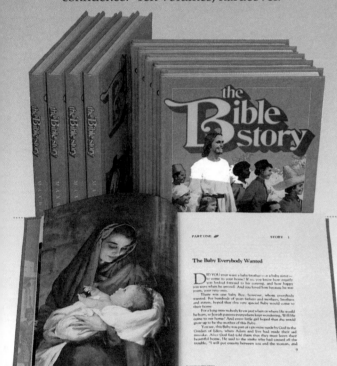

The Desire of Ages
This is E. G. White's monumental best-seller on the life of Christ. It is perhaps the most spiritually perceptive of the Saviour's biographies since the Gospel According to John. Here Jesus becomes more than a historic figure—He is the great divine-human personality set forth in a hostile world to make peace between God and man. Two volumes, hardcover.

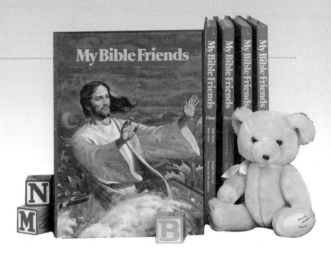

Uncle Arthur's Bedtime Stories
For years this collection of stories has been the center of cozy reading experiences between parents and children. Arthur Maxwell tells the real-life adventures of young children—adventures that teach the importance of character traits like kindness and honesty. Discover how a hollow pie taught Robert not to be greedy and how an apple pie shared by Annie saved her life. Five volumes, hardcover.

FOR PRESCHOOL CHILDREN
My Bible Friends
Imagine your child's delight as you read the charming story of Small Donkey, who carried tired Mary up the hill toward Bethlehem. Or of Zacchaeus the Cheater, who climbed a sycamore tree so he could see Jesus passing by. Each book has four attention-holding stories written in simple, crystal-clear language. And the colorful illustrations surpass in quality what you may have seen in any other children's Bible story book. Five volumes, hardcover. Also available in videos and audio cassettes.

For more information, write: The Bible Story, P.O. Box 1119, Hagerstown, MD 21741.

MORE FAMILY READING

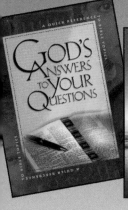

God's Answers to Your Questions
You ask the questions; it points you to Bible texts with the answers

He Taught Love
The true meaning hidden within the parables of Jesus

Jesus, Friend of Children
Favorite chapters from *The Bible Story*

Bible Heroes
A selection of the most exciting adventures from *The Bible Story*

The Storybook
Excerpts from Uncle Arthur's *Bedtime Stories*

My Friend Jesus
Stories for preschoolers from the life of Christ, with activity pages

Quick and Easy Cooking
Plans for complete, healthful meals

Fabulous Food for Family and Friends
Complete menus perfect for entertaining

Choices: Quick and Healthy Cooking
Healthy meal plans you can make in a hurry

More Choices for a Healthy, Low-Fat You
All-natural meals you can make in 30 minutes

Tasty Vegan Delights
Exceptional recipes without animal fats or dairy products

Fun With Kids in the Kitchen Cookbook
Let your kids help with these healthy recipes

Health Power
Choices you can make that will revolutionize your health

Secret Keys
Character-building stories for children

Winning
Gives teens good reasons to be drug-free

FOR MORE INFORMATION:
- mail **the attached card**
- or write
  Home Health Education Service
  P.O. Box 1119
  Hagerstown, MD 21741
- or visit **www.thebiblestory.com**